THE ULTIMATE GUIDE TO
HORSES

THE ULTIMATE GUIDE TO
HORSES

Debby Sly

PaRragon

Bath · New York · Singapore · Hong Kong · Cologne · Delhi · Melbourne

First published by Parragon in 2009

Parragon
Queen Street House
4 Queen Street
Bath BA1 1HE, UK

Copyright © Parragon Books Ltd 2009

All rights reserved. No part of this publication may be
reproduced, stored in a retrieval system, or transmitted, in any
form or by any means, electronic, mechanical, photocopying,
recording, or otherwise, without
the prior permission of the copyright holder.

Created and produced by

13 SOUTHGATE STREET WINCHESTER HAMPSHIRE SO23 9DZ

DESIGN Sharon Rudd
EDITORIAL Jennifer Close

ISBN: 978-1-4075-5530-0

Printed in China

STUDIO CACTUS WOULD LIKE TO THANK
Sharon Cluett for original styling; Jo Weeks for proofreading;
and Penelope Kent for indexing

PICTURE CREDITS
All images © Kit Houghton/Houghton's Horses except:
Alexia Khruscheva 10 crb, 10 br, 11 cra, 56 b, 73 br; Animal
Photography 9 tr; Bob Langrish 16–17 c, 83 tr, 83 bl; 11 crb;
Claudia Steininger; Condor 36 11 br; Craig McAteer 26 b;
cynoclub 91 bl; Daniel Gale 80 bl; Eline Spek 10 tr, 37, 46 bl, 90
tr, 90 bl; Filipchuk Oleg Vladimirovich 6; Graca Victoria 20 bl; J.
Helgason 87 tr; Jean Frooms 11 tr; Jeff Banke 32 br; Joy Brown
21 cr; Kondrashov MIkhail Evgenevich 30 bl, 31 b, 69 bl, 69 br;
Laila Kazakevica 36 bl; Lee O'Dell 35 b; Lincoln Rogers 25 br;
Lorraine Kourafas 8 b; Michaela Steininger 85 b; Neil Roy
Johnson 71 br; NHPA 14–15 l; Otmar Smit 10 cra; Petr Masek 66
b; Shutterstock.com 2–3, 34 tr, 57 br; Studio Cactus 20–21 c,
24–25 c, 26–27 c, 28 tr, 28 bl, 28–29, 32 bl, 35 tr, 67 bl, 67 br, 77
b, 78 t, 78 b, 79 tl, 79 br, 80–81 c, 82 tr, 82 b, 84 tl, 84 bl, 86 tl,
86 br, 88 b, 89 tl, 89 br, 91 t, 92 tr, 93 tr, 93 bl, 94 tr.

Cover credits: Main Image: White Arab stallion © Lothar Lenz/
zefa/Corbis. Right hand side/back image: sunset © Getty
Images. Bottom left to right: Friesian © Eline Spek; Danish
Warmblood © Kit Houghton/Houghton's Horses; Palomino ©
Kit Houghton/Houghton's Horses

GOOD LEGS

The horse's limbs should be well aligned, well balanced, and well proportioned. A picture of perfection is hard to find: Many highly successful performance horses have conformational faults and different horsepeople develop their own ideas of exactly what they are looking for in a horse. The legs should be well proportioned from shoulder to hoof, with a pastern and hoof angle of 45 degrees. Pasterns, in particular, should be well proportioned: Too long and they put excessive strain on the tendons and

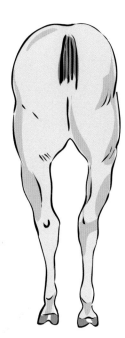

HINDQUARTERS The quarters should be well rounded and powerful and allow the hind legs to be well positioned, showing a balanced line from the point of the buttock to the hock and to the floor.

ligaments; too short and they produce too much concussion. Viewed from the side, the legs should not appear to tilt forward (over at the knee) or backward (back at the knee).

A GOOD HEAD

The horse's head should have a wide forehead. It should be well placed on a powerful, well-proportioned neck. The head should join the neck in a way that doesn't restrict the windpipe and therefore the horse's ability to breathe efficiently. The neck should be set on the shoulders in a way that will make it natural and comfortable for the horse to carry himself well. A low-set neck makes it harder for the horse to lighten and elevate his forehand. The shoulders should be at an angle of about 45 degrees. Too steep an angle limits the horse's ability to open out his stride.

GOOD CHEST

A broad chest indicates plenty of heart room and gives the horse more powerful movement of his front legs. The back should be straight and not too long or too short. Ideally, the measurement from wither to croup should be the same as the length of neck from poll to wither.

GOOD FEET "No foot no 'oss" is an old saying. The hooves should have the strength, size, and shape to carry the weight of horse and rider.

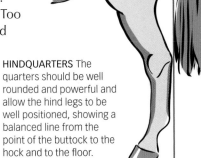

BREED CATALOGUE

Horses are traditionally divided into three categories, according to their proportions and origins. Heavy horses, with a build suitable for strenuous draft work, are the giants of the equine world. These coldbloods derive from the primitive Forest Horse of northern Europe, and are generally slow moving and short limbed. Light horses, longer limbed and built for agility and speed, have their origins in hotbloods, often with an injection of cold blood many generations back to create warmbloods. These versatile breeds have been used for a variety of purposes from light draft work to sport. Finally, ponies, standing at under 14.2 hh (58 in), make up for in spirit what they lack in inches. Largely evolving in colder northern climes and often in harsh terrain, they are noted for their stamina and hardiness.

EQUINE EVOLUTION The horse we recognize today evolved from a small, fox-sized creature that inhabited the earth over 55 million years ago. The species has been developed and refined and is now represented by over 200 different breeds.

Ardennais

ORIGIN France/Belgium

ENVIRONMENT

BLOOD

USES

HEIGHT 15.3–16.1 hh (63–65 in)

COLORS Mostly roan, but also gray, chestnut, bay, brown, and palomino

BROWN	CHESTNUT	GRAY	BAY	PALOMINO	ROAN

The relatively short but incredibly powerful Ardennais is named after its homeland, the rugged Ardennes region on the French/Belgian border. It is an ancient breed; its ancestors were praised for their stamina and toughness by Julius Caesar 2,000 years ago. The heavy type is known as the "carthorse of the north."

ORIGINS

The Ardennais is believed to be the direct descendent of the Solutrian Horse: A prehistoric, snub-nosed horse that lived over 50,000 years ago whose skeletal remains were discovered at Solutré, southeast France. Evidence suggests that the Solutrian horse stood at about 15 hh (60 in), as does the smaller type of Ardennais. These horses roamed in a cold, mountainous region and they evolved to be surefooted and tough.

RIDING HORSE

Prior to the 19th century, the breed was not as massive and thickset as it is today, and it was used for riding as well as for draft work. Some were ridden in the crusades, and when Arab horses were brought back to Europe during the crusades, their finer blood was crossed with that of the Ardennais. During the 17th and 18th centuries, much use was made of the breed in battle. It is said that Napoleon owed his safe return from the Russian campaign to them.

In the early 19th century, more Arab and Thoroughbred blood was introduced, as well as some Boulonnais and Percheron. The relatively small Ardennais that proved his worth as a cavalry and artillery horse is now quite rare but Ardennais blood is very evident in other breeds. The demands of

RED ROAN The most common and popular color for the Ardennais is roan, particularly red roan. Iron gray is acceptable but not dapple gray, and chestnut, palomino, bay, and brown are also allowed.

agriculture for a strong workhorse led to outcrosses to the larger Belgium Draft. This produced the more commonly found heavy Ardennais, and influenced the development of the Trait du Nord, sometimes known as the Ardennais du Nord, and the Auxois.

CHARACTERISTICS

The Ardennais is short and stocky, with a thickset neck, a short back, and muscular loins. His limbs are short with plenty of bone. The feet are relatively small but strong. There are thick, wavy feathers on the lower limbs, although the original, smaller Ardennais has slightly lighter bones and less feathering. The head is short and blunt. The Ardennais is kind, willing, and gentle. For such a massively powerful beast, he is surprisingly energetic and active.

FARM WORK The Ardennais has studbooks in a number of European countries and efforts are made by its breed societies to encourage the horse's use in farming and forestry work.

Boulonnais

ORIGIN Northwest France

ENVIRONMENT

BLOOD

USES

HEIGHT 15.0–16.2 hh (60–66 in)

COLORS Predominantly gray, but also bay, black, and chestnut

| BLACK | CHESTNUT | GRAY | BAY |

The Boulonnais, sometimes called the White Marble Horse, is the most elegant of the heavy horses, largely due to Arab influence in its bloodlines. Once widespread in France, the stock was devastated in the World Wars. All Boulonnais have an anchor-shaped brand on their necks to honor their coastal origins.

ORIGINS

The heavy type of Boulonnais that exists today is a direct descendant of the knight's charger. A smaller, lighter type, known as the Mareyeur (horse of the tide) was used to haul the heavy carts of fish from Boulogne to Paris. The journey covered 200 miles (322 km) and could be made in under 18 hours, allowing fresh fish to be delivered in time for breakfast in Paris. The breed's strength, endurance, and speed made him the ideal transporter. An annual race, the *Route du Poisson*, is still held today to commemorate the horse. The smaller type has all but disappeared and while the large Boulonnais does find some employment in agriculture, he is mainly produced for his meat.

Much is being done to preserve the Boulonnais, however, including the creation of the American Boulonnais Horse Association, which is working with French breeders to develop a breeding population of Boulonnais horses in the United States.

CHARACTERISTICS

The Boulonnais has a good, rounded rib cage, a perfectly set shoulder, and well-placed withers. There is very little hair on the powerful limbs with their solid clean joints, open hocks, and short cannon bones. The neck is thick and muscular, with a thick double mane. He has a short, elegant head with a wide, flat forehead.

EXPRESSIVE FACE The Oriental blood in his ancestry shows in the large, dark eyes, expressive face, and sharp, mobile ears. He has a gracefully arched neck and good sloping shoulders.

GOOD PACES The Boulonnais has exceptionally good paces for a heavy horse. His action is straight and long, and his paces swift and energetic. His limbs are strong but not as heavily feathered as they are in many draft breeds.

Clydesdale

ORIGIN Scotland

ENVIRONMENT

BLOOD

USES

HEIGHT 16.2–17.0 hh (66–68 in)

COLORS Commonly bay, but also black, brown, gray, roan, and chestnut

BLACK

BROWN

CHESTNUT

GRAY

BAY

ROAN

The Clydesdale proved a popular heavy draft breed and was extensively exported from his native Scotland. He is described by the Clydesdale Horse Society as being "handsome, weighty, and powerful, with a gaiety of carriage and outlook.... The impression given being of quality and weight rather than grossness and bulk."

ORIGINS

The Clydesdale as a recognized breed came into being in the 19th century but was most likely descended from a type of draft horse being developed during the 18th century. During that time a horse breeder, called John Paterson from Lochyloch in Scotland, bought a big black Flemish horse from England to cross with the local native stock of packhorse. The stallion stamped his stock well and the Lochyloch bloodline became much in demand. The horses he bred were similar to the modern Clydesdale and were often marked with a lot of white. In 1808, a stallion called Thompsons Black Horse, or Glancer, was in popular use and he was believed to be of Lochyloch blood. Glancer can be traced in many Clydesdale pedigrees. Shire blood was also used to create what we now recognize as the Clydesdale. Often referred to as Scotland's Shire Horse, the Clydesdale is less massively built and is a better mover than the Shire. In 1877, the Clydesdale Horse Society was launched but even before this large numbers

DRIVING HORSE The Clydesdale's gaiety of character and movement makes him a popular choice as a driving horse. Thanks to this, and a continuing enthusiasm for showing the breed, he has a more assured future than some of the other heavy draft breeds that have found themselves mainly unemployed since the middle of the last century.

SOUND Clydesdales are selectively bred for good limbs and feet, giving the breed a reputation for soundness. It is acceptable for this breed to have "cow hocks"— hocks that point inward.

WHITE MARKS Broad, white face markings are a characteristic of the breed, along with plenty of white on the legs and often splashes of white around the belly. Big, kind eyes and big ears add to the attraction of this gentle giant.

of Clydesdales were being exported as far afield as the United States, Australia, and New Zealand. Many Clydesdales were conscripted for army use in World War I. As with all the heavy breeds, his place of power on farms and in cities was quickly usurped by tractors and trucks as the mid-19th century woke up to engine power.

CHARACTERISTICS

The Clydesdale Horse is a picture of power without bulk. His neck is longer than that of the Shire, giving him a slightly rangier look. The withers are well defined and the powerful shoulders gently sloping. An attractive characteristic of the Clydesdale, which adds to his showiness, is the abundance of white markings on the lower limbs, sometimes extending right up the legs and around the belly, and the characteristic white face. He has fine feathering on his lower limbs and round, open feet. Renowned for his soundness, the Clydesdale is currently enjoying a revival of interest and remains popular for showing, driving, farm work, and even riding.

Irish Draft

ORIGIN Ireland
ENVIRONMENT
BLOOD ◊
USES
HEIGHT 15.2–16.3 hh (62–67 in)
COLORS All solid colors

Irish men, women, and their horses are renowned for being great "crossers of the country": Irish horses, and the Irish Draft crosses in particular, are among the most sought-after hunters anywhere in the world. The influence of the Irish Draft has been hugely beneficial in the development of sports horses.

BLACK	BROWN	CHESTNUT	GRAY	BAY

ORIGINS

The ancestors of the Irish Draft breed were brought to Ireland by the Normans as war horses during the Anglo-Norman invasion of 1172. These were probably French and Flemish draft horses that were then bred with the smaller native stock. Some refinement was added in the 16th century with the introduction of Andalucian and, possibly, Arab blood. The early Irish Draft was smaller on average than the horse we know today, and heavier in stature. He had to be a multipurpose beast, able to work on the farm, either plowing or carting, and able to be ridden when necessary, which to an Irishman, meant hunting.

The horse became renowned for his common sense and "sixth leg" when crossing the country, making him a comfortable and safe mount.

THOROUGHBRED

The Great Famine of 1845–49, followed by a general agricultural recession, saw thousands of these horses slaughtered. In the 1900s, when agriculture had begun to thrive again in Ireland, Clydesdales and

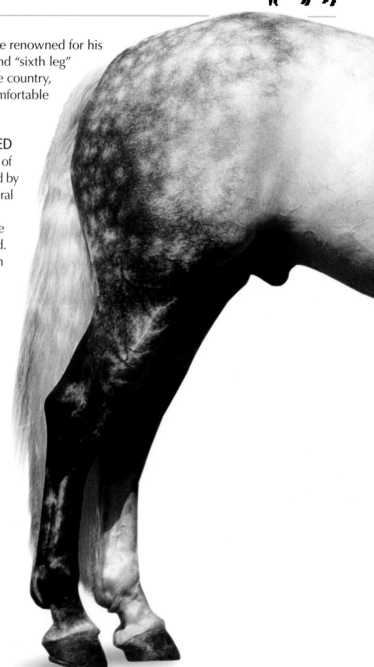

BRUSH WITH EXTINCTION The pure Irish Draft was in danger of dying out by the middle of the 20th century. The Irish Draft Horse Society was formed in 1976 to preserve and promote the breed.

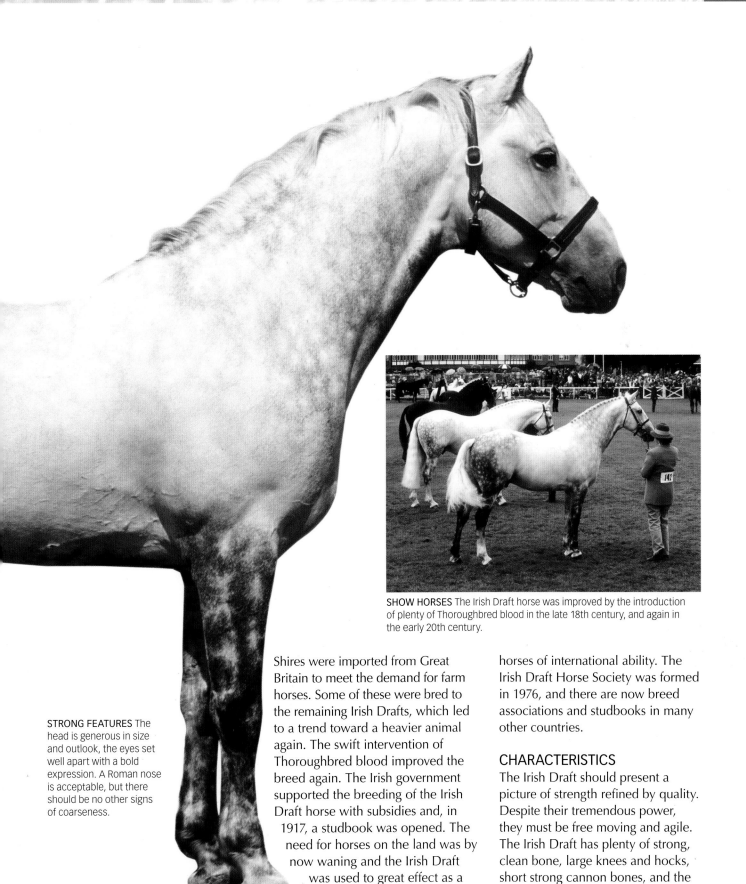

SHOW HORSES The Irish Draft horse was improved by the introduction of plenty of Thoroughbred blood in the late 18th century, and again in the early 20th century.

STRONG FEATURES The head is generous in size and outlook, the eyes set well apart with a bold expression. A Roman nose is acceptable, but there should be no other signs of coarseness.

Shires were imported from Great Britain to meet the demand for farm horses. Some of these were bred to the remaining Irish Drafts, which led to a trend toward a heavier animal again. The swift intervention of Thoroughbred blood improved the breed again. The Irish government supported the breeding of the Irish Draft horse with subsidies and, in 1917, a studbook was opened. The need for horses on the land was by now waning and the Irish Draft was used to great effect as a crossbreed to produce sports horses of international ability. The Irish Draft Horse Society was formed in 1976, and there are now breed associations and studbooks in many other countries.

CHARACTERISTICS

The Irish Draft should present a picture of strength refined by quality. Despite their tremendous power, they must be free moving and agile. The Irish Draft has plenty of strong, clean bone, large knees and hocks, short strong cannon bones, and the feet of a hunter, and not a carthorse!

Percheron

ORIGIN France

ENVIRONMENT

BLOOD ◊

USES

HEIGHT 15.2–17.0 hh (62–68 in)

COLORS Predominantly dapple gray or black, but occasionally chestnut, bay, or roan

| BLACK | CHESTNUT | GRAY | BAY | ROAN |

The Percheron, despite his massive size, was greatly influenced as a breed by the delicate—by comparison—Arab horse. Similarly, Arab influence was important in the development of the Boulonnais and both these breeds reflect a combination of size, strength, and quality.

ORIGINS

The breed developed in Le Perche in the south of Normandy. It is thought that it descends from the heavy warhorses that carried the knights of Charles Martel who defeated the Muslims at Poitiers in 732AD. Whether or not this was the case, this defeat of the Muslims delivered into the hands of the French a large number of Barb and Arab horses. These were bred to the heavy horses and a further influx of Arab blood followed the First Crusade in 1099. Normandy itself has long been an important horsebreeding region and, during the 18th century, Arab stallions were again made available to local breeders by the stud at Le Pin. Two particularly influential Arab sires were Godolphin and Gallipoly, the latter siring one of the most important foundation Percheron stallions, Jean le Blanc, around 1830.

CHARACTERISTICS

The Arab gave to the Percheron great soundness and stamina, as well as the attractive refined head, good action, and clean legs. These qualities, combined with his size and strength, made him a popular draft horse, not only in his native France but also around the world, with the U.S.A. and Canada proving to be a huge market for the breed. They were used for farm work, riding, and carriage work. Sadly, Percherons served in their thousands in World War I.

The Percheron has a particularly beautiful head for such a massive horse. He has a broad forehead; large, dark, expressive eyes; large but fine ears; and large, open nostrils. The neck is long and

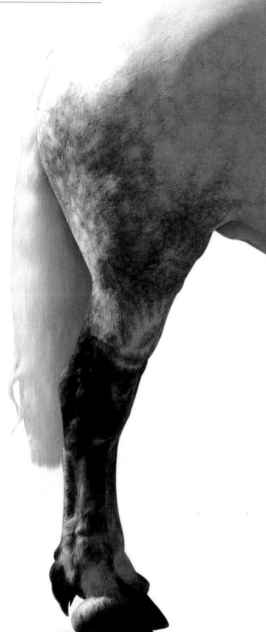

POLICE HORSE Not an obvious choice for a riding horse perhaps, but it is easy to see the temptation: His good conformation, particularly through the withers, shoulder and neck, allow him to carry a rider well. He makes a formidable police mount.

gracefully arched and set well onto large, sloping shoulders.

The back is short and strong, there is great depth through the girth, and his ribs are well sprung. His hindquarters are well sloped and have good length. So many attributes contribute to his open, free paces, which help make him such an elegant horse. He is sometimes crossed with the Thoroughbred to produce a quality heavyweight hunter.

REFINED POWER The Percheron presents a picture of refined power. He has none of the obvious coarseness about him that is seen in some of the other draft breeds. His amenable temperament and adaptability to different climates made him a hugely popular export.

BIG IN AMERICA Although the breed is predominantly gray, the black Percheron found great favor in North America, where the large, heavier stamp of horse was preferred.

Shire Horse

ORIGIN United Kingdom
ENVIRONMENT
BLOOD ◊
USES
HEIGHT 16.2–18.0 hh (66–72 in) or more
COLORS Commonly black, but also brown, gray, and bay

BLACK   BROWN   GRAY   BAY

The Shire Horse is the largest of the heavy horses in the U.K. With his massive size and weight he is truly a gentle giant, much loved for his docile, generous nature. His name derives from the fact that he was bred in the middle "shires" of England: Lincolnshire, Leicestershire, Staffordshire, and Derbyshire.

ORIGINS

Picture an armored knight upon his charger, and you will find yourself looking at the forefather of the Shire. The Medieval Great Horse came to England with William the Conqueror in 1066. He was bred to be strong enough to carry an armored knight complete with heavy weapons, and yet have the agility to move out of danger or "in for the kill" during the confusion of battle.

The introduction of firearms saw the end of his use as a war horse and his strength was put to use in heavy draft work, plowing the land or pulling carts and wagons. During the 17th century, Flemish blood was added to the mix as a result of Dutch workers bringing their own draft horses to the east of England. As time went on another import, the Friesian, was crossbred to give the emerging "Black Horse," as he was known, better movement. In the Midlands of England, more selective breeding led by Robert Bakewell resulted in the Shire Horse that we recognize today.

STILL POPULAR

Today, Shire Horses are still used for beer and bread deliveries, and even for street cleaning and garbage collecting. Recently, the Shire Horse Society has been encouraged by the promising results of a feasibility study to reintroduce the pulling power of

FARM WORK Shire Horses are still used on some farms and are given the chance to show off their working skills at plowing matches. The horse brasses seen decorating the harness were once believed to ward off evil.

FOAL A Shire foal can grow up to over 18 hh, and will weigh approximately 2,205 lb (1,000 kg) when fully mature. A resurgence of interest in the use of genuine horsepower means he may well grow up to have a serious job to do.

MAMMOTH Shires are famed for their massive build. The tallest horse ever recorded was a Shire called Sampson. He was born in 1846 in Bedfordshire, England, and grew to stand at 21.2 hh (84 in), weighing 1½ tons (1,524 kg). As he grew he was renamed Mammoth!

the Shire for both commercial and leisure barges on canals. Also, the Shire's strength and size make him a popular cross with Thoroughbred mares to produce an impressive weight-carrying riding horse or hunter.

CHARACTERISTICS

The Shire's average height is 17.2 hh (70 in) and his girth measurement can vary from 6 ft (1.8 m) to 8 ft (2.4 m). The head is long and lean with a slightly Roman nose and large, kind eyes. He has a good length of neck, set into deep shoulders that must be wide enough to carry a harness collar. His back is short, strong, and muscular, especially over the loins. The hindquarters are long and sweeping, and very well muscled. Although he should be broad across the chest and hindquarters, his hocks must be carried quite close together. His lower legs should display the characteristic feathers, which should be fine, straight, and silky. As with any workhorse his feet should be, and generally are, very strong, wide, and well shaped.

Suffolk Punch

ORIGIN United Kingdom

ENVIRONMENT

BLOOD

USES

HEIGHT 16.0–16.3 hh (64–67 in)

COLORS Only chestnut, seven shades of which are recognized by the breed society

The Suffolk Punch is Britain's oldest heavy horse breed and his "roly-poly" shape makes him an easily recognized and very endearing horse. All Suffolk Punch horses are "chesnut" in color, the word being spelt without the first "t" in all Suffolk breed records.

ORIGINS

The Suffolk Punch originated in East Anglia, in England. A unique feature of the breed is the fact that every Suffolk Punch can trace its lineage back to a single stallion: Thomas Crisp's horse of Ufford, which was foaled in the 1760s. The exact origins of this particular stallion are not known, but it is highly likely that the Flanders Horse, brought to East Anglia by Dutch workers in the 17th century to help to drain the fenlands, was instrumental in its development. Also likely to have had some influence on the development of the breed is the Norfolk Roadster, a popular trotting horse that was bred at the time.

BRAIDED TAIL The mane and tail of the Suffolk Punch are traditionally braided. The tail, as with most draft breeds, is braided or tied up to keep it out of the way of the mud and machinery.

RARE BREED The Suffolk Punch suffered greatly as a result of the mechanization of farming. In 1966 only nine foals were born. Great efforts have been made to restore its numbers with the establishment of several breeding programs, but it remains rare.

CHARACTERISTICS

The horse was bred to work the heavy clay soils of East Anglia, so a strong, but clean legged animal was needed. The breed is instantly recognizable by its color (any one of seven shades of chesnut) and its shape. It has an adorably big, round body set on relatively short legs. The head is large with small ears. The renowned pulling power of the horse starts with the deep neck set well onto long, low, muscular shoulders. The low set of the shoulders is a characteristic that has been carefully retained by breeders. The quarters have great width and strength, but the hind legs must be close set so that the horse can walk between rows of crops without causing excessive damage.

INTELLIGENT HEAD Suffolks have intelligent-looking heads with active ears, and powerful necks that are clean-cut at the throat. The mane is decorated for show purposes.

HOT TO TROT The Suffolk Punch is also a good trotter, making him a popular choice for carriage as well as draft work; testimony to the Norfolk Roadster and Flanders blood in his pedigree.

Akhal-Teke

ORIGIN Turkmenistan
ENVIRONMENT
BLOOD
USES
HEIGHT 14.3–16.0 hh (59–64 in)
COLORS Commonly chestnut, but also black, dun, gray, bay, and palomino

| BLACK | CHESTNUT | DUN | GRAY | BAY | PALOMINO |

The Akhal-Teke is a distinctive horse in terms of shape and color. His coat, whatever the color, has a truly metallic sheen to it. The horse is a picture of athleticism, although his long back and rather tubular body would be considered poor conformation by some. Like the Arab, he has remarkable powers of endurance.

ORIGINS

The true origins of the breed are not exactly known. Some argue that he is an older breed than the Arab, others that the Arab is the forefather of the Akhal-Teke. He closely resembles what we call Horse Type 3: One of the four subspecies of horses and ponies that had developed around the time that horses were first being domesticated.

TOUGH HORSE Courage, endurance, and toughness are breed characteristics. Although the Akhal-Teke is said to have a tricky temperament, the Turkmen people obviously understood the breed well, as the horses were renowned for being devoted to their owners.

LEGENDARY ENDURANCE In 1935, a group of Akhal-Teke horses were ridden from Ashkabad in Turkmenistan to Moscow in Russia. A distance of over 2,500 miles (4,000 km) was covered in just 84 days.

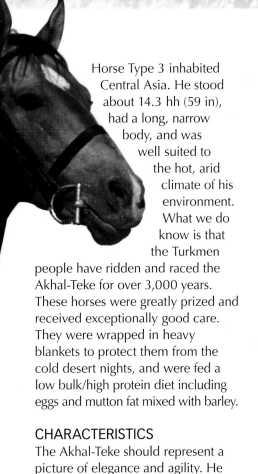

Horse Type 3 inhabited Central Asia. He stood about 14.3 hh (59 in), had a long, narrow body, and was well suited to the hot, arid climate of his environment. What we do know is that the Turkmen people have ridden and raced the Akhal-Teke for over 3,000 years. These horses were greatly prized and received exceptionally good care. They were wrapped in heavy blankets to protect them from the cold desert nights, and were fed a low bulk/high protein diet including eggs and mutton fat mixed with barley.

CHARACTERISTICS

The Akhal-Teke should represent a picture of elegance and agility. He has a fine head, with large expressive eyes and long, beautifully shaped ears. His neck is long, elegant, and high set. The back is long and the body can be tubular looking. The legs are long, slender, and quite close set, but the breed is renowned for his toughness and stamina. The mane and tail are fine and silky, often with no forelock, and the coat color carries a striking metallic sheen. This effect is due to the structure of the hairs, which have a very thin outer layer. This allows the core of the hair to act like a light tube that dramatically reflects the light, so affording some protection from the searing desert heat. Today, the Akhal-Teke is used as a racing horse, both for speed and endurance, and also competes in jumping and dressage.

RACING BREED Akhal-Tekes were traditionally used for racing, and the sport still flourishes. However, they are also popular as riding and sports horses, particularly for dressage and show jumping.

American Saddlebred

ORIGIN United States

ENVIRONMENT

BLOOD 🌢

USES

HEIGHT 15.0–16.0 hh (60–64 in)

COLORS Black, chestnut, gray, bay, palomino, and roan

Left in his natural state, the American Saddlebred horse is a fine riding and harness horse. He was originally bred to be a good all-purpose animal, but refinements made for the show ring, such as an unnatural tail carriage and unusually long hooves, have led to him being looked upon by some as rather artificial.

| BLACK | CHESTNUT | GRAY | BAY | PALOMINO | ROAN |

ORIGINS

In the early 19th century, settlers in the southern states of America set about breeding a horse that would be elegant but practical. He had to carry a man for many hours over rough terrain to inspect crops, he had to be smart enough to pull a carriage, and he had to be tough enough to work cattle. His main bloodlines include two pacer breeds: The now-extinct Narrangansett Pacer and the Canadian Pacer, as well as the Thoroughbred.

CHARACTERISTICS

He has unique paces and is trained to be either a three- or five-gait horse. Three-gait Saddlebreds work in walk, trot, and canter, with all three paces being slow, collected, and elevated. The five-gait horse also shows a high-stepping slow gait and the "rack"—a fast, flashy four-beat gait. The hooves are grown very long and shod with heavy shoes to exaggerate the gaits.

QUALITY HEAD The head carries many of the same qualities of a Thoroughbred: cleanly defined lines, alertly pricked ears, and a proud, bold, and intelligent expression.

OUTLINE The Saddlebred's distinctive outline features a high set, long, arched neck; a short, strong back; and a level croup. The artificially induced tail carriage is clearly illustrated here, as are the long hooves and big, heavy shoes.

Andalucian

ORIGIN Spain
ENVIRONMENT
BLOOD ◊
USES 🐎 🏇 🐎 🏇
HEIGHT 15.0–15.2 hh (60–62 in)
COLORS Gray or bay

GRAY   BAY

The Andalucian was, for centuries, known as the Spanish Horse. He was a much admired and coveted animal, taken as a spoil of war and used in many countries to improve the native stock. Spanish Horses were the foundation stock of many American breeds, having been taken to the Americas by the Spanish *conquistadores* in the 16th century.

ORIGINS
The Andalucian originated in southern Spain and most likely evolved through crossing North African Barbs with native pony stock (possibly Sorraia Ponies). Before the last Ice Age, there was a land bridge (now the Straits of Gibraltar) between North Africa and Spain, which would have made this possible. During many turbulent periods of war, the Andalucian owed its survival to the monasteries. The Carthusian monks of Jerez were particularly conscientious about maintaining the best bloodlines.

CHARACTERISTICS
The Andalucian is a handsome, proud breed, which, although not overly tall, is compact and muscular. They have great spirit and courage, but are also gentle and exceptionally trainable. The big, lofty paces and the powerful hindquarters with particularly flexible hocks make the breed adept at High School work. They are also used for bullfighting.

GRAY COLORATION Gray is the predominant color of the breed, and the horses always have a particularly luxuriant, and often wavy, mane and tail.

Appaloosa

ORIGIN United States
ENVIRONMENT 🌿
BLOOD 💧
USES 🏇 🐎
HEIGHT 14.2–16.0 hh (58–64 in)
COLORS Colored

Spotted coat coloring has been found in horses for thousands of years; cave drawings from 20,000 years ago depicted horses with these coats. In the United States, the word "Appaloosa" refers to a breed of spotted horses, but the word can also refer simply to the coat color.

ORIGINS

Spotted coat coloration featured on many of the horses reintroduced to the Americas by the *conquistadores* in the 16th century, and the Appaloosa breed was developed in the 18th century by the Nez-Perce Indians. This tribe lived in Palouse country, the area that is now north Idaho and Oregon—a fertile stretch of country that includes the Palouse River. They selectively bred their horses to promote the spotted coat coloring that they so prized. The horses became known as Palouse Horses which, over time, changed to Appaloosa Horses. The defeat of the Indians by the U.S. army in the late 19th century very nearly led to the loss of this type of horse. Many were killed in the fierce fighting; those that survived escaped to run wild. In the

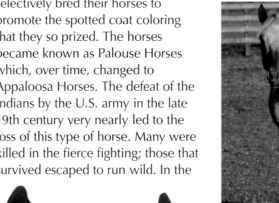

VARIED BREED As a breed, Appaloosas are usually strong, compact horses, although because the breed is defined by color rather than bloodlines, they can vary tremendously both in size and shape. They are popular for Western and endurance riding as well as for general competition classes.

INTELLIGENT BREED The Appaloosa often has a thin mane and tail, white sclera around the eye, and mottled skin, particularly around the eyes, muzzle, and genitalia. They are usually intelligent and cooperative, despite the white around the eye suggesting otherwise.

1920s, the breed was revived by enthusiasts breeding from the descendants of the Indian ponies.

SPOT THE DIFFERENCE

While all Appaloosas have spots, there are five officially recognized coat patterns: Blanket, with a spot free area of white over the hips; Frost, with white specks in a dark coat color; Leopard, with a predominantly white area over the loins and hips featuring large dark spots within the white; Marble, with a mottled pattern all over the body; and Snowflake, with a white body covered all over in dark spots, but the spots being particularly prevalent over the hips.

CHARACTERISTICS

The Appaloosa has a generally sparse tail and mane, which was encouraged to avoid snagging on thorn bushes in its native environment. White sclera around the eyes and mottling on the muzzle is also characteristic. (Too much white around the eye is considered a poor character trait by many horse people, but in the Appaloosa it is a breed requirement.) The limbs are notably strong, and the hooves are good and hard, often with distinctive vertical stripes. The Nez-Perce Indians never shod their horses.

HORSE CLUB
The Appaloosa Horse Club was formed in 1938 in Oregon. Their aim was to preserve and improve the Appaloosa breed as well as to act as a register for Appaloosa horses.

BLANKET SPOT There are five different Appaloosa coat patterns. This foal would be classed as a Blanket spot if this white area over his hips remains spot free. His coat may change as he matures and, if spots appear on the white, he would be classed as a Leopard spot.

Arab

ORIGIN Middle East
ENVIRONMENT
BLOOD
USES
HEIGHT 14.2–15.0 hh (58–60 in)
COLORS All solid colors

The Arab is the oldest and purest of all horse breeds, and also one of the most beautiful and distinctive. Believed by many to be a gift from God, "fashioned from the desert wind," a horse that "could fly without wings," the Arab is also the forefather of the Thoroughbred.

| BLACK | BROWN | CHESTNUT | DUN | GRAY | BAY |

ORIGINS

The exact origins of the breed are unknown, but the Bedouin tribe who religiously guarded the breeding of their "desert horse" trace him back as far as 3000BC to a mare called Baz, said to be have been captured in Yemen by Bax, "the great-great-grandson of Noah."

The Bedouin people put great value on their Arab mares, breeding only from the very best and passing down from generation to generation the pedigrees and dam lines that they prized the most. The Arab Horse was introduced to other parts of the world—the rest of the Middle East, North Africa, China, and Europe—as a result of the Muslim conquests, started in 600AD. By the 1700s, the Arab Horse had found his way into Asia and North America. Everywhere he went, his blood was used to refine and improve that of the native breeds.

MARENGO

A gray Arab called Marengo was the favorite charger of Napoleon Bonaparte. Marengo was captured by the British after the Battle of Waterloo in 1815. When he died, his skeleton was displayed in the National Army Museum.

CHARACTERISTICS

Arabs are generally around 15 hh (60 in) and are well proportioned, elegant, and athletic. Stamina and soundness were attributes valued by the nomads who nurtured this breed, and this has given them a natural edge, allowing them to excel in endurance riding. A unique skeleton defines the distinctive shape: it has 17 ribs, 5 lumbar, and 16 tail vertebrae. Others breeds have an 18–6–18 bone arrangement. The neck is arched and the head is set at an angle that allows great mobility. A unique feature of the head is the jibbah, a shield-shaped bulge between the eyes.

DISHED PROFILE The Arab's head is very distinctive. It has a broad forehead and a slightly dished profile. The nostrils are large and the eyes are set low and wide. The ears are small and may curve inward.

ELEGANT SHAPE The Arab's back is short and concave, the loins are strong, and the croup long and level. The tail is high set and carried high and arched.

Barb

ORIGIN North Africa
ENVIRONMENT
BLOOD
USES
HEIGHT 14.2–15.2 hh (58–62 in)
COLORS Solid colors; commonly black, brown, gray, and bay

BLACK   BROWN   GRAY   BAY

The Barb is little used outside his native North Africa, and yet he has had almost as great an influence as a foundation bloodline as the Arab. He played a major role in the development of both the Andalucian and the Thoroughbred. He has the qualities of the Arab, but not its refined looks.

ORIGINS

It is possible that the Barb was one of a small group of horses that survived the Ice Age. This would make the breed older than the Arab. Certainly, his primitive head lends credence to him being an ancient breed.

The coastal region of Morocco, Algeria, and Tunisia known as the Barbary coast was home to the Barb horse. The spread of Islam, and hence the arrival of a Muslim army in Europe in the early 8th century, saw the spread of the Barb Horse also. He was the mount of the Berbers, who led the early Muslim conquests, invading Spain in 711AD.

In modern times, the most famous use of Barb horses was in the Algerian and Tunisian cavalry regiments of the French Army.

CHARACTERISTICS

The Barb is remarkably quick and agile. Although the head has a straight profile, unlike that of the Arab, the neck is distinctly arched. The legs are slender and very hard, and the hooves are extremely tough.

SPRINTING HORSE The Barb Horse can show tremendous speed over short distances, and this is dramatically exhibited during the wild, rifle firing charges that feature in many North African festivals.

STRAIGHT PROFILE Unlike the Arab, the Barb has a straight or even convex profile.

Belgian Warmblood

ORIGIN Belgium

ENVIRONMENT

BLOOD 🜂

USES

HEIGHT 16.0–16.2 hh (64–66 in)

COLORS Black, brown, chestnut, gray, and bay

Belgian horse breeders had made a great success of producing heavy, dependable draft horses but are relative newcomers to the art of producing a sports horse, only beginning the project in the 1950s, when the calm after the storm of war allowed thoughts to turn to such luxuries.

BLACK   BROWN   CHESTNUT   GRAY   BAY

ORIGINS

In the 1950s, a heavyweight riding horse had been developed by crossing some of the light Belgian farm horses to the Gelderlander. The result was nothing much more than a reliable weight-carrying riding horse. There was then a period of outcrossing to a number of breeds, including the Thoroughbred, Arab, and the neighbouring Dutch Warmblood. The result was a horse with sufficient speed, scope, and stamina to meet the demands of equestrian sports but with a good, calm temperament.

CHARACTERISTICS

The breed has retained the soundness and strength of its heavy draft forefathers and has good paces with a degree of elevation but not the spectacular movement of some of the other warmblood breeds.

CAREFUL MIX Strong hindquarters and loins, sound limbs, and good overall proportions are the result of the careful mix of breeding that has produced the Belgian Warmblood.

STRONG JUMPER The breed has been able to put its power to good use in show jumping, his trainable temperament also being an asset in a sport that demands an accurate technique.

Brumby

ORIGIN Australia
ENVIRONMENT
BLOOD
USES
HEIGHT 15.0–16.1 hh (60–65 in)
COLORS All solid colors

Brumbies are the feral horses of Australia, with numbers in their thousands. Those who love them see them as a symbol of the wilderness and freedom of Australia; others see them as a pest, causing damage to the environment and eating up resources that are needed for cattle and sheep.

BLACK BROWN CHESTNUT DUN GRAY BAY

ORIGINS

The Brumbies that roam free today are the descendants of horses that were either lost by, or escaped from, the early European settlers. The first horses imported into Australia were Cape Horses from South Africa. Later, there were shipments of Chilean horses as well as ponies and draft horses from Britain. The occasional Thoroughbred or Arab also joined the "mob" or "band," as a herd of Brumbies is known. From this diverse early mix of bloodlines, the harsh, unforgiving environment and landscape of Australia—through natural selection—created the tough, cunning, wiry little horse that is the Brumby.

HARD TIMES

Today, Brumbies are found mainly in Queensland and the Northern Territory. Their successful survival has led to conflict with farmers and conservationists and since the 1960s, they have been culled, although this has been banned in some states after a gruesome cull when hundreds were shot from helicopters, causing mass panic and injuries as well as death.

SANCTUARY After the controversy raised by culling methods, some were offered sanctuary by sympathetic landowners and others are captured and offered for "adoption."

Canadian Cutting Horse

ORIGIN Canada
ENVIRONMENT
BLOOD 💧
USES 🏇 🏇
HEIGHT 15.2–16.1 hh (62–65 in)
COLORS All solid colors but generally brown, chestnut, gray, or bay

Cattle ranching is big business in Canada, and large numbers of horses are still used for ranch work. Canada does not have any indigenous horse breeds, but it does have a thriving horse-breeding industry. The Canadian Cutting Horse has evolved from this industry to meet the needs of the ranch owners.

BLACK   BROWN   CHESTNUT   DUN   GRAY   BAY   PALOMINO

ORIGINS
The main aim of the Canadian Cutting Horse Association is to promote the sport of cutting cattle—separating a specified animal from a herd. The Association does not have a closed studbook, so the bloodlines of the horse are not specified. It is left to the horse to prove he has the necessary attributes to cut cattle.

CHARACTERISTICS
Most Canadian Cutting Horses carry a high percentage of Quarter Horse blood. In turn, the Quarter Horse evolved from the Spanish Horse, from which both these breeds inherit their "cow sense."

In cutting competitions, once the selected cow is split from the herd, the rider drops the reins and leaves the horse to "mark" the cow and prevent it rejoining the herd. The horse's agility, stamina, and intelligence enable it to outmaneuver the cow.

CONFORMATION The well-proportioned head is set on a gently arched neck. The shoulders are sloping and powerful, the chest broad and deep, and the hindquarters immensely powerful.

Cleveland Bay

ORIGIN United Kingdom
ENVIRONMENT
BLOOD
USES
HEIGHT 16.0–16.2 hh (64–66 in)
COLORS Bay

The Cleveland Bay is a very attractive bay horse. Popularly used for carriage driving, he also makes a good hunter, and crosses with the Thoroughbred result in a good stamp of sports horse, particularly for show jumping. The Cleveland Bay is always bright bay, which sets off the black "points" of his legs and the mane and tail.

CARRIAGE HORSE The 18th century was the golden age of carriage driving. The Cleveland Bay was crossed with the Thoroughbred to produce the faster Yorkshire Coach Horse. These exceptional carriage horses were exported all over the world.

ORIGINS

The Cleveland Bay is believed to be Britain's oldest breed, descended from a particular stamp of bay pack horses that were bred in the monasteries of northern England during the Middle Ages. The bay horse they bred was used by traveling tradesmen, known as "chapmen," and the horse became known as the Chapman Horse.

CHARACTERISTICS

In the 17th century, the Chapman Horse was crossed with Barb and, in some cases, Andalucian horses. The result, which became known as the Cleveland Bay, was a strong but elegant horse with a level, free, long striding action, which could be used for riding, carriage, and light draft work.

BOLD AND HONEST An active, elegant but very powerful horse, the Cleveland Bay is bold and honest, but he has a strong character, which can make him difficult if mishandled.

Colorado Ranger

ORIGIN United States
ENVIRONMENT
BLOOD
USES
HEIGHT 14.2–16.0 hh (58–64 in)
COLORS Predominantly Appaloosa, but all colors accepted

| BLACK | BROWN | DUN | GRAY | BAY | PALOMINO |

The Colorado Ranger is a relatively new breed: The result of a breeding program aimed at producing a good cowhorse. Most Rangers have Appaloosa colorings, but while many are double registered with Appaloosa breed societies, the Colorado Ranger is not a type of Appaloosa.

ORIGINS AND CHARACTERISTICS

In 1878, two stallions were given to General Grant by the Sultan of Turkey: An Arab called "Leopard" and a Barb called "Linden Tree." Two descendants of these stallions, "Patches" and "Max," became the foundation stock of the Colorado Ranger. They were bred to working mares on the ranges of Colorado, and their offspring were popular for their often striking spotted colors, agility, and intelligence. Registered horses are all directly descended from either Patches or Max.

OFFICIAL BREED The Colorado Ranger Horse Association was formed in 1935, and keeps meticulous handwritten records of the pedigree and coat pattern of each horse.

Criollo

ORIGIN Argentina
ENVIRONMENT
BLOOD
USES
HEIGHT 14.0–15.0 hh (56–60 in)
COLORS Predominantly dun, but also chestnut

| CHESTNUT | DUN |

The Criollo is a famously tough, hardy little horse, shaped by the harsh environment of the pampas of Argentina. The extremes of climate—hot, arid summers and severe winters—insured the survival of only the soundest and fittest.

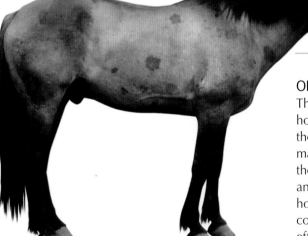

VERSATILE Originally used as a riding and pack horse, the Criollo is also the chosen mount of the gauchos for herding cattle. Crossed with the Thoroughbred, it produces a superb Polo Pony.

ORIGINS AND CHARACTERISTICS

The Criollo descends from Spanish horses taken to South America by the *conquistadores*, which were mainly Andalucian Horses. Many of these early imported horses ran wild and formed feral herds. A very tough horse emerged. Dun is the most common color and provides effective camouflage.

Danish Warmblood

ORIGIN Denmark

ENVIRONMENT

BLOOD 🜄

USES 🐎 🏇

HEIGHT 15.3–16.2 hh (63–65 in)

COLORS All solid colors

The Danish Warmblood is a relative newcomer to the band of purpose-bred breeds developed across Europe to meet demand from the sports horse industry. The Danes have a long horse-breeding history, but their native breeds, the Frederiksborg and the Knabstrup, are not sports horses.

BLACK   BROWN   CHESTNUT   GRAY   BAY   PALOMINO

ORIGINS AND CHARACTERISTICS

A breeding program with the aim of developing a sports horse was started in 1962. Local mares were bred to a selection of Swedish, Trakehner, Holsteiner, and Polish stallions to start the process. Strict grading procedures were then introduced to insure that only the best mares and stallions were entered in the studbook. The end result is a good-looking, courageous horse with excellent paces—a successful competition horse that excels particularly in dressage.

BRANDED All Danish Warmbloods are branded with a crown and an identification number on their hindquarters once they are accepted for registration in the breed's studbook.

DRESSAGE Like all warmbloods, the Danish Warmbloods are bred to produce an all-round performer. Warmbloods are popular for dressage due to their extravagant action.

Dutch Warmblood

ORIGIN Holland

ENVIRONMENT

BLOOD

USES

HEIGHT 16.0–17.0 hh (64–68 in)

COLORS All solid colors but mainly bay and brown

BLACK   BROWN   CHESTNUT   GRAY   BAY

The Dutch have proved adept at producing horses to meet market demands, and the Dutch Warmblood has probably been the most successfully marketed of all the warmblood breeds. The product has lived up to its reputation with some excellent competition horses, particularly in dressage and show jumping.

ORIGINS

The Dutch already had a smart carriage horse in the form of the Gelderlander, and the heavier Groningen, and these two breeds were the starting point for the Dutch Warmblood. Thoroughbred blood was used to correct an overly long back and also greatly influenced the head and neck. Trakehner stallions were also used, as well as Holsteiner mares crossed to the Gelderlander and Groningen stallions. As the basic type was formulated, further warmblood breeds were used to add the final touches.

CHARACTERISTICS

A strict selection process is used to grade and accept Dutch Warmbloods. The main aim, of course, is to continue to produce horses of good conformation and movement but, just as importantly, the breed society aims to retain good temperament and trainability. The Thoroughbred influence shows in the elegant head and neck. The Gelderlander helps to produce the good shoulder and active paces, and the Groningen insures strength, particularly in the hindquarters, and soundness.

VERSATILE While the carriage horse past makes this a good competition driving horse, the breed is better known for its huge successes in show jumping—"Marius" and his famous son "Milton"—and in dressage—"Dutch Courage."

Friesian

ORIGIN Holland
ENVIRONMENT ▲
BLOOD 🌢
USES 🐎 🏇 🐎
HEIGHT 15.0–16.0 hh (60–64 in)
COLORS Black

The Friesian is a striking little horse: Strongly built, jet black, with an abundant wavy mane and tail. Originally he was used for light farm work, but today he is more likely to be employed as a carriage and riding horse, particularly for dressage. He is sometimes called a funeral horse since he is a popular choice for horse-drawn hearses.

ORIGINS

The Friesian descended from an ancient coldblooded heavy horse that inhabited Friesland in northern Holland. The breed was noted and used by the Romans and was improved with the introduction of Arab blood at the time of the crusades and Andalucian blood from the Spanish occupation of the Netherlands during the Eighty-Year War. During the 19th century, some crosses were also made with Trotting breeds, the result being a slightly lighter framed horse. In turn, the Friesian has influenced other breeds, such as the Fell Pony and the Oldenburg. After World War I, the breed went into decline, but fuel shortages during World War II saw

HIGH STEPPER The active, high stepping trot of the Friesian makes him a popular carriage horse. Here he is shown drawing a traditional gig. He is still used to some degree to work the land but is increasingly popular for leisure activities.

a resurgence of interest in the breed as he was brought back to work the land and provide transportation.

CHARACTERISTICS

The Friesian has a long but attractive head and an arched neck. The back is short and broad, and the shoulders and hindquarters are powerful. The limbs are short, with plenty of bone and some feathering. The hooves are blue horn. The full mane and tail come from his Andalucian ancestors.

BLACK BEAUTY The jet black coloring of the Friesian—combined with his striking mane and tail, and kind, easy nature—makes him a popular choice for a number of disciplines. The breed has great presence, which adds to his appeal as a carriage horse in particular.

Gelderlander

ORIGIN Holland
ENVIRONMENT
BLOOD
USES
HEIGHT 15.3–16.2 hh (63–66 in)
COLORS Predominantly chestnut, but also gray and bay

CHESTNUT   GRAY   BAY

The Gelderlander was developed by the breeders of the Gelder province in central Holland. Their aim had been to produce an upstanding carriage horse that was strong enough to undertake light draft work too but which retained a docile temperament.

ORIGINS AND CHARACTERISTICS

Gelderlanders were developed in the 19th century using various European stallions on Dutch mares. The result has been a successful carriage horse popularly used for four-in-hand driving trials. The horse also excels as a showjumper and was a major influence in the development of the Dutch Warmblood.

SENSIBLE HORSE The Gelderlander has a plain but kind and sensible head, a strong neck, and very good shoulders. The hindquarters are powerful with a highset tail.

Gidran Arab

ORIGIN Hungary
ENVIRONMENT
BLOOD
USES
HEIGHT 16.0–16.2 hh (64–66 in)
COLORS Nearly always chestnut

BROWN   CHESTNUT   BAY

The Gidran Arab is also known as the Hungarian Anglo-Arab and was another breed to be developed at the famous Mezohegyes stud. The breed was developed during the 19th century and produced two lines: A light draft horse and a faster riding horse.

ORIGINS AND CHARACTERISTICS

The chestnut Siglavy Arab stallion "Gidran," imported into Hungary in 1816, was bred to a Spanish mare, producing "Gidran II"—the breed's foundation sire. Local and Spanish mares were used initially and then, increasingly, only Arab and Thoroughbred, both of which have left their mark.

TRICKY The original stallion Gidran was notorious for his "tempestuous" temperament. This trait has been passed to his offspring in varying degrees.

Hackney Horse

ORIGIN United Kingdom
ENVIRONMENT 🌿
BLOOD 💧
USES 🐎
HEIGHT 15.0–15.3 hh (60–63 in)
COLORS Solid dark colors

The high-stepping Hackney Horse is instantly recognizable and, although a native of Great Britain, is prized throughout the world as an eye-catching carriage horse. Hackney carriage turnouts are very popular in the show ring, and the Hackney can be driven as a single horse or in teams of two, three, or four.

BLACK   BROWN   CHESTNUT   BAY

ORIGINS
The Hackney has his early origins in the 1700s as a general-purpose type used for riding, hunting, and light farm work. The horses were highly regarded and valued by the monarchy of the time; Henry VIII passed an act penalizing anyone who exported one of these horses without permission!

HIGH-STEPPING ACTION The exaggerated high-stepping action is inherited from his Trotting horse ancestors. A small version of the Hackney Horse, the Hackney Pony, also exists.

In 1883, the Hackney Studbook Society was formed and a studbook was opened. During the early 20th century, Hackneys were exported in large numbers all over the world.

CHARACTERISTICS
The Hackney should express alertness and activity. The head has a straight or slightly convex profile with intelligent, wideset eyes. The body should have good depth and well-sprung ribs. The quarters should be well muscled and the chest should have ample width.

CLEAN LIMBS The limbs have plenty of clean, flat bone with sufficiently long pasterns to provide the characteristically light, springy step.

Hanoverian

ORIGIN Germany
ENVIRONMENT
BLOOD ◊
USES
HEIGHT 15.3–16.2 hh (63–66 in)
COLORS Mainly chestnut and bay

The Hanoverian was bred to be an all-purpose horse capable of working the land, being ridden, and also suited to carriage work. More recently, the emphasis has been on refining the breed for the sports industry. The Hanoverian now suits this purpose very well and is especially popular for dressage and show jumping.

BLACK	BROWN	CHESTNUT	GRAY	BAY

ORIGINS

The Hanoverian breed was produced at the state stud at Celle, in Germany, after 1835. Here, Thoroughbred stallions were crossed to mainly Holsteiner mares. The Hanoverian Breed Registry was founded in 1888, and in 1922 became the Hanoverian Horse Breeders Association. After 1945 more Thoroughbred and Trakehner blood was used.

CHARACTERISTICS

Modern Hanoverians should have a quality head set on a long, elegant neck. The shoulders are large and well sloped, and the back not too long, with especially strong loins and muscular hindquarters. The limbs are strong with well-defined joints.

NOBLE BEARING
The Hanoverian's strength and noble bearing, combined with his powerfully active paces, makes him a good choice for the controlled power and athleticism required for top level dressage.

WELL TESTED Hanoverian breeding is strictly controlled. Stallions can only be licensed after passing a veterinary examination and must then prove their ability in ridden performance tests. Great emphasis is placed on the horse's temperament, which is considered to be as important as its athletic ability.

Kathiawari

ORIGIN India
ENVIRONMENT
BLOOD
USES
HEIGHT 15.0 hh (60 in)
COLORS All solid colors except black

The Kathiawari breed is found mainly on India's northwestern coast, and is named after the Kathiawar Peninsula of that region; he is also found in Maharashtra, Gujerat, and southern Rajasthan. Both the Kathiawari and its near neighbor, the Marwari, have unique and remarkably shaped, inward-curving ears.

BROWN   CHESTNUT   DUN   GRAY   BAY

ORIGINS
Native horses of steppe and desert origin had roamed this region of India for centuries. Some were ancient breeds such as the Kabuli and Baluchi, from which it is thought the Kathiawari inherited the distinctive ears. From the

CURVED EARS The most notable feature of the breed is the uniquely shaped ears; these touch each other at the tips and can rotate through nearly 360 degrees.

1500s, during the reign of the Moghul Emperors and, later, during the rule of the British Raj, Arab horses were imported, as were Cape Horses from South Africa. These were bred to the native stock to produce the Kathiawari. The breed was a favorite of Indian royalty, and was bred at the royal palaces. During the 19th century, it was employed as a cavalry horse and is still used by mounted police forces in India.

CHARACTERISTICS
The Kathiawari resembles the Arab in many ways. He is slightly light of bone but is inherently sound.

Lipizzaner

ORIGIN Slovenia

ENVIRONMENT

BLOOD ◊

USES

HEIGHT 15.1–16.2 hh (61–66 in)

COLORS Generally gray, but also black and bay

BLACK	GRAY	BAY

The Lipizzaner is known to most people through the classical riding demonstrations of "Haute École" given by the Spanish Riding School of Vienna, but it also makes an excellent driving horse. It is bred in several countries that were once part of the Austro-Hungarian empire.

ORIGINS AND CHARACTERISTICS

During the late 16th century, some excellent horses were bred in Spain by crossing the best Arab bloodlines to the athletic and elegant Spanish horses. Some of these horses were taken to Austria and used at the newly formed Kladrub stud. A second stud was formed at Lipizza in Slovenia, with the aim of producing riding horses. The Kladrub stallions "Maestoso" and "Favory" became two of the foundation sires of the Lipizzaner. During the 18th and 19th centuries a mixture of Spanish, Italian, and Arab blood was used. The resultant breed is distinguished by his powerful hindquarters, which enable him to perform the demanding high school movements.

HIGH CARRIAGE Lipizzaner horses also make excellent carriage horses. A larger, free moving stamp of Lipizzaner is bred in Hungary, and this is particularly well suited to driving work.

Lusitano

ORIGIN Portugal
ENVIRONMENT
BLOOD
USES
HEIGHT 15.0–16.0 hh (60–64 in)
COLORS Predominantly gray and bay

The Lusitano takes its name from the word "Lusitania," which is the Latin name for Portugal. It is very like the Andalucian of neighboring Spain and shares a similar history. Classified together as the Iberian Horse, both are believed to have evolved from the Sorraia Pony and the Barb.

| BLACK | BROWN | CHESTNUT | DUN | GRAY | BAY | PALOMINO |

ORIGINS AND CHARACTERISTICS

It is believed that selective breeding from the 18th century onward created the difference between the two breeds. The greatest influence is said to have been the introduction of bullfighting on foot in Spain, whereas in Portugal, the bullfighters continued on horseback.

The Lusitano is an exceptionally courageous and agile horse, traits born of the talents required to outmaneuver an enraged bull. His head is long and noble, often with a convex profile. He looks "leggier" than the Andalucian, mainly due to overly long cannon bones.

CONFORMATION The Lusitano is a well-conformed horse, as would be expected of an animal required to show the elevation and collection required for dressage work, as well as the overall agility needed in the bullring. He carries an abundant and wavy mane and tail.

SPANISH WALK The Lusitano horse is used for the competitive discipline of dressage as well as for classical High School work. This horse is demonstrating the Spanish Walk, an exaggerated and extended walking gait.

Morgan

ORIGIN United States

ENVIRONMENT

BLOOD

USES

HEIGHT 14.1–15.3 hh (57–63 in)

COLORS All dark colors, no white leg markings permitted above the knee or hock

BLACK   BROWN   CHESTNUT   BAY

The foundation sire of the Morgan Horse breed is a legend. Of unknown breeding, he found fame for his courage, strength, speed, and indomitable spirit despite his tiny stature. Originally called Figure, his name was changed to that of his owner, Justin Morgan.

ORIGINS AND CHARACTERISTICS

Justin Morgan was foaled in 1789 and may have been a mixture of Dutch, Arab, and Thoroughbred blood. Only 14 hh (56 in), he was lightweight and full of quality. He worked hard for 30 years, plowing, hauling, and even racing. An exceptional sire, he passed his qualities to his offspring.

FINE BREEDING Morgans have a fine, expressive face, an arched neck, strong, sloping shoulders, and well-defined withers. His long pasterns aid his light springy step.

Mustang

ORIGIN United States

ENVIRONMENT

BLOOD

USES

HEIGHT 14.0–15.0 hh (56–60 in)

COLORS All colors

BLACK   BROWN   CHESTNUT   DUN   GRAY

The Mustang is the feral horse of North America. Of Spanish descent, it mixed with other breeds that escaped over the years. In the early 19th century, numbers were estimated at over two million. Widespread culling took place until the horses were protected by an act passed in 1971.

ORIGINS AND CHARACTERISTICS

In the 16th century horses from Spain of Arab, Andalucian, and Barb blood were introduced to North America by the *conquistadores*. Many escaped to run wild, and the native American Indians kept them in large numbers. Over time, horses of any number of breeds joined the herds, creating much variation in type. However, they all shared traits necessary for survival: Soundness, hardiness, and cunning.

TOUGH The Mustang is found in a variety of types and all colors. They are tough and very trainable. The Bureau of Land Management, which is responsible for these horses, offers captured Mustangs for rehoming, but there is a shortage of homes.

Missouri Foxtrotter

ORIGIN United States

ENVIRONMENT

BLOOD 🟆

USES

HEIGHT 14.0–16.0 hh (56–64 in)

COLORS All colors, but predominantly chestnut

The Missouri Foxtrotter was developed out of a need for settlers in Missouri to have a horse that could comfortably travel for many miles over the rugged terrain of the Ozark Hills. Although named and most famous for its "foxtrot," the Foxtrotter has two other distinctive gaits: The flat foot walk and a "rocking horse" canter.

BLACK   BROWN   CHESTNUT   DUN   GRAY   BAY

ORIGINS

Early settlers crossed the Mississippi River and began to make their homes in Missouri in the early 1800s. They came mainly from Tennessee, Virginia, and Kentucky, and brought with them various saddle horses such as Morgans, Thoroughbreds, and Spanish horses. These were interbred to produce a horse best suited to the rugged terrain of this area. Some use of the American Saddlebred as well as the Tennessee Walker helped produce the Missouri Foxtrotter. His defining gait is best described as walking with the front legs and trotting with the hind legs.

Any jarring or concussion is eliminated in the way that the horse places his hind feet; they touch the ground and slide forward to follow the tracks of the front feet. Moving in this way, the horse can maintain a speed of up to 8 mph (13 kph) over considerable distances.

The early breeders were able to develop a horse with this natural gait without losing the equally important traits of soundness, stamina, and a gentle and kind temperament. The Missouri Foxtrotting Horse Breed Association was founded in 1948. A fire destroyed the original

THE FOXTROT The gait after which the horse is named is comfortable and efficient, allowing horse and rider to travel over difficult terrain with minimum exertion. The horse walks with the front legs and trots with the hind legs, sliding them forward as the feet touch the ground to follow in the tracks of the front feet.

studbook and records, and the association was reformed in 1958. There are well over 40,000 registered Missouri Foxtrotters in Canada and America.

CHARACTERISTICS
The breed has developed into a muscular, compact horse that is particularly versatile. In comparison to the Tennessee Walker and American Saddlebred, which influenced its development, the Missouri Foxtrotter has

COMPACT The Foxtrotter is not as showy as the Tennessee Walker or the American Saddlebred. He looks more of a workhorse with his powerful, compact body, and his relatively low outline. He is renowned for his stamina and overall soundness.

a relatively low outline and lower action. The head can be a little plain, although it is neat and clean and tapers to a narrow muzzle. The expression is alert and intelligent. The chest is wide and deep, and the shoulders sloped and powerful—the movement coming from the shoulders rather than from any exaggerated knee action. The hindquarters, too, are powerful and muscular with a lowset tail.

PLEASURE RIDING The kind, gentle temperament and the comfortable gait of the Missouri Foxtrotter makes him a popular choice for pleasure and trail riding. There are also specialist showing classes for the breed. His size and temperament make him a suitable mount for both adults and children.

Oldenburger

ORIGIN Germany
ENVIRONMENT
BLOOD 💧
USES
HEIGHT 16.0–17.2 hh (64–70 in)
COLORS All solid colors, but usually black, brown, or gray

BLACK	BROWN	CHESTNUT	GRAY	BAY

Bred since the 1600s, the Oldenburger is the heaviest of the German warmbloods. The birthplace of the Oldenburger was an area near what is now Lower Saxony, near the city of Oldenburg. The horse was developed from a mixture of breeds but was heavily influenced by the Friesian in particular.

ORIGINS

Count Johann XVI von Oldenburg set up several stud farms in the late 16th century using a good mix of stallions, mainly to produce carriage horses.

POWERHOUSE The Oldenburger is the largest and heaviest of Germany's warmblood breeds. But he is very well made and certainly not a cumbersome animal.

His successor also used a variety of stallions of Polish, Barb, and English blood. In 1861 the Oldenburg studbook and branding was introduced. The breed society followed in 1897. With the arrival of mechanization, breeders refined the Oldenburger to obtain a performance horse, using Thoroughbreds among others.

CHARACTERISTICS

The head is relatively plain, but the expression is kind. The hind limbs and quarters are strong—this is the powerhouse that is such an asset for dressage and show jumping.

Orlov Trotter

ORIGIN Russia
ENVIRONMENT
BLOOD
USES
HEIGHT 15.3–16.0 hh (63–64 in)
COLORS All solid colors, but predominantly gray

The Orlov Trotter is one of Russia's oldest breeds, and is one of the three most successful trotting breeds in the world, the others being the American Standardbred and the French Trotter. The Orlov is now not so well known outside his homeland, but is important in Russian harness racing.

BLACK   BROWN   CHESTNUT   GRAY   BAY

ORIGINS AND CHARACTERISTICS

The Orlov Trotter takes its name from Count Alexis Orlov. During the late 1700s, he imported a gray Arab stallion called "Smetanka." One of his offspring was another gray stallion called "Polkan I" who was bred to a Danish mare to produce "Bars I," foaled in 1784. Bars I was a successful sire and the foundation stallion of the Orlov Trotter.

The head of the Orlov Trotter is small with a broad forehead and alert, pricked ears. His neck is high set, and swan-like, giving him an elegant bearing. The back is long but strong, with muscular loins.

FOUNDATION SIRE Because of the close inbreeding program that was used to produce the definitive stamp that characterizes the Orlov Trotter, the pedigrees of purebred Orlovs all trace back to the foundation sire, Bars I.

THE TROIKA A popular harness set-up in Russia is the Troika. The center horse maintains a trot while the outrunners canter to keep pace. Each outrunner is made to carry its head and neck to the outside.

Palomino

ORIGIN United States
ENVIRONMENT 🌾
BLOOD 💧
USES 🏇 🏇
HEIGHT 14.0–17.0 hh (56–68 in)
COLORS Light, medium, or dark gold

The word "palomino" properly describes a coat color rather than a breed. Many different breeds can produce palomino horses, but in America, the "color" has become virtually accepted as a breed through the Palomino Horse Association and the Palomino Horse Breeders Association.

ORIGINS

The Palomino coat color has been depicted in the ancient art of Europe and Asia, as well as featuring in Japanese and Chinese artefacts since 200BC. These horses were ridden by the Arabs and the Moors and, during the crusades, a "splendid Golden Palomino warhorse" was presented to Richard *Coeur-de-Lion* by the Emir Saladin. Queen Ysabella de Bourbon of Spain was an enthusiastic breeder of Palominos, and it is reported that she sent a Palomino stallion and five brood mares out to New Spain (as newly discovered Mexico was known) so that the "breed" could be developed in the New World. The idea of registering Palominos as a type began in 1935 when Dick Halliday registered his Palomino stallion "El Rey de los Reyes." He was a "golden-

ALL SORTS The Palomino Horse Association now accepts cream colored horses with blue eyes since they produce palomino offspring.

horse" enthusiast, and his subsequent articles inspired breeders to specialize in producing horses with this coat color. The original register was incorporated into the newly formed Palomino Horse Association in 1936.

CHARACTERISTICS

The Palomino Horse Association accepts any breed provided it meets their conformational and color requirements. The ideal palomino coloring is described as being that of a newly minted gold coin, with shades varying from light, medium, to dark palomino. The mane and tail should be white, silver, or ivory, with no more than 15 percent dark hairs.

STRIKING GOLD There is no denying that the palomino coloring is striking. The origins of the name are not known, but it may derive from a certain Don Juan De Palomino who was given a "golden horse" by the *conquistador* Hernán Cortés.

Paso Fino

ORIGIN Puerto Rico and Columbia
ENVIRONMENT
BLOOD
USES
HEIGHT 13.2–15.2 hh (54–62 in)
COLORS All colors

The Paso Fino is a naturally gaited horse developed from the Spanish Jennet, the Barb, and the Andalucian. *Paso* means "step" and *fino* means "fine," providing a good description of the breed's defining features. It is said that speeds of up to 16 mph (26 kph) can be achieved with the rider in total comfort.

BLACK   BROWN   CHESTNUT   DUN   GRAY   BAY   PALOMINO   COLORED

ORIGINS AND CHARACTERISTICS

The foundation stock of this breed was taken from Spain to what is now the Dominican Republic and, as Spanish settlers continued to explore the New World, on into Puerto Rico, Columbia, Cuba, and Mexico. The Paso Fino exhibits three natural gaits. The *classic fino* is the slowest of the gaits and is usually only seen in show horses. The *paso corto* is a working trot with good, ground-covering strides. The *paso largo* is an extended trot, which can achieve the same speed as a canter.

WELL BALANCED The Paso Fino has developed as a well-balanced horse in every sense of the word. Conformationally, he is well proportioned, handsome, and full of quality.

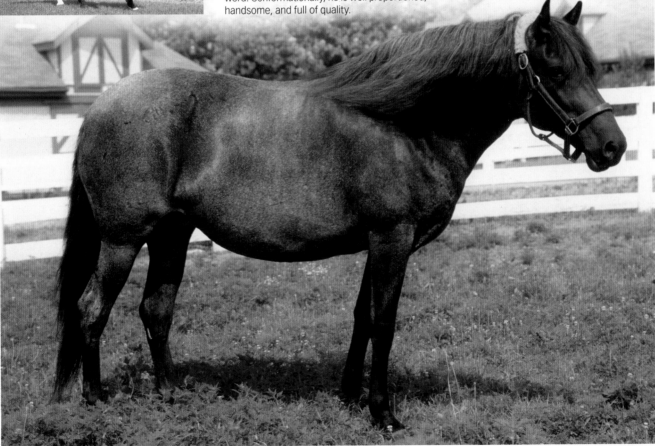

Peruvian Paso

ORIGIN Peru
ENVIRONMENT
BLOOD
USES
HEIGHT 14.1–15.2 hh (57–62 in)
COLORS All solid colors including dun, palomino, and roan

Horses were brought to Peru by the Spanish *conquistadores*, and it was a mixture of Spanish Jennet, Barb and Andalucian blood that gave rise to the Peruvian Paso—the "National Horse of Peru." Its origins are similar to those of the Paso Fino, but it is quite distinct.

BLACK   BROWN   CHESTNUT   DUN   GRAY   BAY   PALOMINO   ROAN

ORIGINS AND CHARACTERISTICS

Three of the breeds imported from Spain in 1532 produced the Peruvian Paso. The smooth, ambling gait came from the Spanish Jennet, the strength and stamina from the Barb, and the conformation, beauty, and action from the Andalucian. It differs from the Paso Fino in having the *termino* action (similar to the arms of a human swimmer in the crawl) and greater extension. It is guaranteed to transmit its gaits to its offspring.

FAST Now mainly employed for pleasure riding and showing, in the past the Peruvian Paso's extended paces allowed him to carry his rider over mountainous terrain at speed.

INHERITED TRAITS The Spanish Jennet has passed on its high-stepping gaits to the Peruvian Paso, a horse that is valued for giving a comfortable ride over rough ground.

Pinto

ORIGIN United States
ENVIRONMENT
BLOOD
USES
HEIGHT 14.2–16.2 hh (58–66 in)
COLORS Broken pattern of white and any other coat color

The Pinto horse covers a multitude of breeds because the word "pinto" refers to the broken coat coloring of the animal. In most countries, pinto is used simply to describe the coat color but in the United States the Pinto Horse is accepted as a breed.

ORIGINS AND CHARACTERISTICS
Pinto Horses descend from Spanish horses introduced to the Americas with the arrival of the *conquistadores* in the 16th century. Although any breed, provided it has the required coat pattern, can register as a Pinto, the stamp of horse is generally that of a stock horse. There are two coat patterns: Overo has a solid coat color as a base with large splashes of white;

Tobiano has a white coat color with large splashes of a solid color. The Pinto Horse Association of America was formed in 1956 and the breed was recognized in 1963. Pinto Horses are registered as stock, hunter, pleasure, or saddle type.

SKEWBALD In many European countries, skewbald describes a coat that is a mixture of white and any color except black.

Plantation Horse

ORIGIN United States
ENVIRONMENT
BLOOD
USES
HEIGHT 14.2–16.0 hh (58–64 in)
COLORS All solid colors, but predominantly gray

In the late 1800s, a family called McCurdy ran a large plantation in central Alabama. In 1905, they bred a fine gray stallion called "McCurdy's Dr. McLain." He was bred to a number of gaited mares, and the breed line, popular with other plantation owners, became known as "the McCurdy."

BLACK   BROWN   CHESTNUT   GRAY   BAY

ORIGINS AND CHARACTERISTICS
All the McCurdy's Plantation Horses were registered as foundation stock for the Tennessee Walking Horse Association in 1930. In 1993 the McCurdy Plantation Horse Association was formed. The breed has a smooth gait, rounded hips, a broad chest, short back, and good bone. It has a thick mane and tail.

McCURDY LICK The four-beat lateral gait of the Plantation Horse is called the "McCurdy Lick."

Polo Pony

ORIGIN Worldwide
ENVIRONMENT
BLOOD
USES
HEIGHT 14.2–16.0 hh (58–64 in)
COLORS All colors

Polo originated in Persia over two-and-a-half-thousand years ago. Polo Ponies can be produced from any mix of light horse and pony breeds, so are a type rather than a breed, but in Argentina, a very set stamp of Polo Pony has been bred by crossing Criollo mares to Thoroughbred stallions.

| BLACK | BROWN | CHESTNUT | DUN | GRAY | BAY | PALOMINO | COLORED |

ORIGINS

The first polo ponies would have been light, Oriental-type horses, the standard mounts of army officers in India and other eastern countries. In the early 20th century the sport was established in Argentina, which quickly achieved dominance due to the players' natural affinity for the game, as well as the quality of the ponies they bred. Up until 1914 there was a 14.1 hh (57 in) height limit, which obviously limited the bloodlines that could be used to produce a Polo Pony. In Britain native ponies were bred to small Thoroughbreds, and, in Argentina, their native Criollos were bred to imported Welsh ponies. Once the height limit was abolished, the Argentines quickly changed tack and bred their Criollos to Thoroughbred stallions and then refined the result further by crossing the resultant half-bred back to a Thoroughbred again.

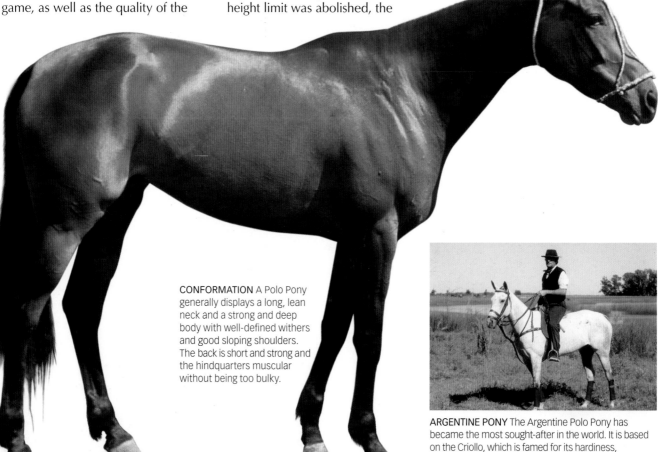

CONFORMATION A Polo Pony generally displays a long, lean neck and a strong and deep body with well-defined withers and good sloping shoulders. The back is short and strong and the hindquarters muscular without being too bulky.

ARGENTINE PONY The Argentine Polo Pony has became the most sought-after in the world. It is based on the Criollo, which is famed for its hardiness, soundness, and stamina.

Quarter Horse

ORIGIN United States
ENVIRONMENT
BLOOD
USES
HEIGHT 14.3–16.0 hh (59–64 in)
COLORS All colors

The Quarter Horse was the first established American breed after horses were reintroduced to the Americas by the *conquistadores*. The breed was primarily a workhorse, but the English settlers brought with them their love of racing, and used it for entertainment in quarter-mile racing—hence the name.

| BLACK | BROWN | CHESTNUT | DUN | GRAY | BAY |

ORIGINS

The origins of the breed lie with the ranchers of 17th-century Virginia, who bred a versatile cow pony using imported English native breeds and local Spanish-type horses. In the mid-1700s, Thoroughbreds were bred to the cow pony, eventually developing the Quarter-Mile Horse, refined to show explosive acceleration over this distance. As the early pioneers headed west onto the great plains during the 1800s, they took Quarter-Mile Horses. Some crossbreeding with the feral Mustangs and Indian ponies enhanced the breed's toughness and cow sense. Further inputs of Thoroughbred blood, plus some Morgan, Arab, and Standardbred followed.

CHARACTERISTICS

The Quarter Horse has a long neck which he carries quite low. He has a broad, deep chest and powerful, well-sloped shoulders, then wide and powerful hindquarters, extending down into well-muscled limbs.

AMERICAN DREAM The American Quarter Horse Association was formed in 1940 by ranchers eager to preserve the dual qualities of cow pony and racehorse. The breed's hugely powerful hindquarters allow it to reach speeds of 45 mph (72.5 kph) over short distances.

Rocky Mountain Horse

ORIGIN United States
ENVIRONMENT
BLOOD
USES
HEIGHT 14.2–16.2 hh (58–66 in)
COLORS Brown or chestnut

BROWN   CHESTNUT

The breed registry of the Rocky Mountain Horse was established in 1986. The breed originates from one gaited colt—the "Rocky Mountain Stallion"—brought from the Rocky Mountain area to the foothills of the Appalachian Mountains in the late 1800s. He was chocolate colored with a flaxen mane and tail.

DISTINCTIVE The breed has a fine, elegant head with a bold eye, and some unusual coloring.

ORIGINS AND CHARACTERISTICS
It is said that the Rocky Mountain Stallion was crossed with local mares and the line continued eventually becoming the modern Rocky Mountain Horse. Sam Tuttle kept the breed going during World War II, primarily using one stallion called "Old Tobe," who appears in the pedigree of many of these horses.

Russian Trotter

ORIGIN Russia
ENVIRONMENT
BLOOD
USES
HEIGHT 15.3–16.0 hh (63–64 in)
COLORS Black, brown, chestnut, gray, or bay

BLACK   BROWN   CHESTNUT   GRAY   BAY

The Russian Trotter is the successor of the Orlov Trotter, which could not compete with the dominant American Standardbred. It was developed by crossing the Orlov to the Standardbred.

ORIGINS AND CHARACTERISTICS
Selective breeding continued during the late 1800s and early 1900s. In 1950, the breed characteristics were set and continue to improve. The Russian Trotter has a plain, straight head on a long, muscular neck. The shoulders are long and sloping, which gives the stride great reach. The legs are strong with well-defined tendons. The common defect of knock-knee and sickle-hocks allows them to lengthen more easily, an advantage for any racehorse.

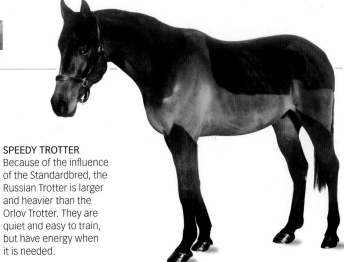

SPEEDY TROTTER Because of the influence of the Standardbred, the Russian Trotter is larger and heavier than the Orlov Trotter. They are quiet and easy to train, but have energy when it is needed.

Selle Français

ORIGIN France

ENVIRONMENT

BLOOD ◊

USES

HEIGHT 16.0 hh (64 in)

COLORS Black, brown, chestnut, gray, or bay

The Selle Français was recognized as a breed in 1958 as a result of the amalgamation of French regional breeds of riding horses that were not Thoroughbred, Arab, or Anglo-Arab. The regional breeds had been classed as halfbloods with pedigrees dating back many generations.

| BLACK | BROWN | CHESTNUT | GRAY | BAY |

ORIGINS

The most popular of the original French regional breeds was the Anglo-Norman. Other regional breeds included the Vendéen Charollais and Angevin. Since the 19th century, the Anglo-Norman was used for crossbreeding with other regional breeds until a characteristic stamp of horse began to be produced.

This became the Selle Français. The Selle Français remains an amalgamation of the regional breeds and falls into three categories: Competition horses, racehorses, and nonspecialist horses that are used in riding schools and for leisure riding. They are also divided into middleweight and heavyweight, according to their weight-carrying ability.

CHARACTERISTICS

A highly courageous horse, he excels in cross-country riding and is a useful driving trials horse. He has a muscular body, large hindquarters, and strong limbs with plenty of bone and well-defined joints. The sloping shoulder gives freedom to his paces.

DISTINGUISHED The Selle Français has a distinguished head with expressive eyes, an intelligent expression, and large ears. Its paces are free and supple.

SECOND DIVISION There are several French races held for horses that are not Thoroughbreds. Horses from this division often make excellent eventers.

Shagya Arab

ORIGIN Hungary

ENVIRONMENT

BLOOD

USES

HEIGHT 15.0 hh (60 in)

COLORS Black, brown, chestnut, gray, or bay

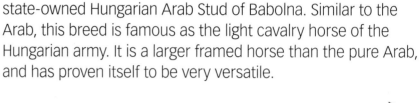

BLACK   BROWN   CHESTNUT   GRAY   BAY

This Hungarian breed, based on the Arab, was developed at the state-owned Hungarian Arab Stud of Babolna. Similar to the Arab, this breed is famous as the light cavalry horse of the Hungarian army. It is a larger framed horse than the pure Arab, and has proven itself to be very versatile.

ORIGINS AND CHARACTERISTICS

The Shagya breed is named after its foundation sire, born in 1830 and taken from the Bedouins. "Shagya" was crossed with local stock that included Arabs, Thoroughbred, Hungarian, and Spanish breeds to produce a stronger stamp of horse. The offspring of these crosses were bred back to Shagya until a distinctive type of horse was established. The result of 150 years of selective breeding has defined this famous cavalry and carriage horse. It is stronger and more versatile than a purebred Arab, and was exported to several countries, including Poland, Austria, and the United States.

The Shagya Arab is a hardy breed that can survive on poor food. It has a very wide forehead with large eyes dominating the typically Arabian dished head, on an elegantly curved neck. The body is well proportioned.

BUILT FOR SPEED The shoulders are sloping, and the body is compact. The legs are set clear of the body, allowing freedom of movement.

SHAGYA HERD Mares and foals are loose housed in large barns at the Hungarian Arab Stud of Babolna. The Shagya Arab conformation is that of the Arab but with a larger frame and substantially more muscle.

Standardbred

ORIGIN United States
ENVIRONMENT
BLOOD
USES
HEIGHT 14.0–16.0 hh (56–64 in)
COLORS All solid colors

The Standardbred is the fastest trotter in the harness racing world, capable of covering 1 mile (1.6 km) in 1 min 55 secs. The breed got its name when it was decided to set a performance standard for horses to gain entry into the Registry, which was founded in 1871.

 BLACK   BROWN   CHESTNUT   GRAY BAY

ORIGINS AND CHARACTERISTICS

The Standardbred was developed mainly from Thoroughbred stock—the most influential sire being "Messenger," who was born in 1780 and can be traced back to the Darley Arabian. Nearly all of today's Standardbreds can be traced back to four of Messenger's sons, one of which, "Hambletonian 10," is classed as the breed's foundation sire. He sired 1,335 offspring between 1851 and 1875. Another influential sire was the Thoroughbred "Diomed," born in 1777.

The Standardbred has very strong legs and very hard hooves; the legs are shorter than those of the Thoroughbred. It is generally more robust in appearance with powerful quarters, and the hind legs are out behind the quarters rather than under.

EARLY STANDARD The early acceptance standards of 2 min 30 secs for trotters and 2 min 25 secs for pacers to cover a mile soon had to be reduced as the breed has became gradually faster and faster. Today, registration is based on bloodlines.

DOMINANT The American Standardbred proved to be such a successful trotter that it has been exported all over the world to improve and upgrade other trotters, with the result that the breed dominates the sport.

Tennessee Walker

ORIGIN United States
ENVIRONMENT
BLOOD
USES
HEIGHT 15.0–16.0 hh (60–64 in)
COLORS All solid colors

Tennessee plantation owners who wanted a horse to ride around their plantation developed this gaited horse in the 19th century. The horse is renowned for its agility, comfortable paces, and swiftness. It is also called the Plantation Walker and the Turn-Row, referring to its ability to turn within the plantation rows.

BLACK   BROWN   CHESTNUT   DUN   GRAY   BAY

THE RUNNING WALK This is the horse's most famous gait. It is a four-beat pace with each foot hitting the ground at regular intervals. The head nods in time and the teeth also click! He can reach speeds of up to 15 mph (24 kph) in the running walk.

ORIGINS
The main foundation stock was the Narragansett Pacer and the Canadian Pacer, both lateral-gaited horses from the colonies. The Standardbred stallion "Black Allen," born in 1886, became one of the most influential sires of this breed. The Tennessee Walking Horse Breeders' and Exhibitors' Association founded the breed registry in 1935, and has successfully promoted the breed with more than 430,000 registered horses throughout the world.

CHARACTERISTICS
The most outstanding characteristics of the breed are the comfortable but unusual gaits: The flat foot walk, running walk, and rocking chair canter. All are natural to the breed. Foals perform the running walk within days of birth.

LONG FEET This close coupled horse is robust, with a short and strong back. The head is large and plain and the croup slopes. Controversially, the front hooves are usually kept long and weighted to increase the elevation and activity of the gaits.

Tersk

ORIGIN Russia

ENVIRONMENT

BLOOD

USES

HEIGHT 14.3–15.1 hh (59–61 in)

COLORS Predominantly gray, but also black, chestnut, and bay

| BLACK | CHESTNUT | GRAY | BAY |

Developed at the Tersk and Stavropol studs during the 1920–40s, this athletic horse is suitable for many purposes, such as endurance and non-Thoroughbred races. It is popular with the Russian Army for riding and harness. It has upgraded other breeds including the Karabakh and Lokai.

ORIGINS

Prior to the Strelet breed becoming extinct, the Tersk stud crossed them with Arabs, Arab-Don crossbreds, Strelet-Karbardin crossbreds, and Shagya Arabs. Selective inbreeding then followed until the required stamp and characteristics became firmly established. The Tersk was officially recognized as a breed in 1948. The aim of the breeding program had been to produce a horse with the best features of the Arab Horse, but with some of the robustness and hardiness of the native breeds.

There are three main types of Tersk—the basic, eastern, and heavy—all descending from five sire lines and five mare families.

CHARACTERISTICS

The head is light and slightly dished, with a broad forehead, and a long poll on a high-set neck. The chest is deep and wide with long sloping shoulders. The croup is rounded and well muscled with clean legs.

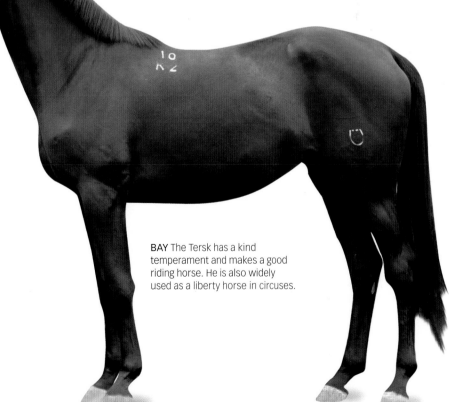

BAY The Tersk has a kind temperament and makes a good riding horse. He is also widely used as a liberty horse in circuses.

NOT FRAGILE The Tersk is usually gray, often with a silvery metallic sheen. It looks fragile, with its thin coat, but survives the harsh Russian winters as an army mount.

Thoroughbred

ORIGIN United Kingdom

ENVIRONMENT

BLOOD

USES

HEIGHT 15.2–17.0 hh (62–68 in)

COLORS All solid colors

The English Thoroughbred is the world's fastest and most valuable horse, forming the basis of the multibillion pound horse racing industry. It is used extensively to improve and upgrade numerous other breeds. The Thoroughbred is the king of the horse breeds: Fast, courageous, and spirited.

BLACK   BROWN   CHESTNUT   GRAY   BAY

ORIGINS

The breed evolved with a certain amount of luck that saw the three founding sires of the breed gathering together in England during the 18th century. English breeders were given a golden opportunity to develop the Thoroughbred racehorse. The three foundation sires were the "Byerley Turk," the "Darley Arabian," and the "Godolphin Arabian." They in turn produced four main Thoroughbred lines: "Herod'," "Eclipse," "Matchem," and a son of Herod called "Highflyer."

The Darley Arabian was brought from Syria by Thomas Darley to stand at stud in Yorkshire in 1704. The Goldolphin Arabian came from Yemen and found his way into the ownership of Lord Godolphin, who stood him in England. The Byerley Turk was captured in battle by Capt. Byerley who then rode him in the Battle of the Boyne in 1690, before sending him to England for stud duties. These Arabian sires were bred to native English stock, many of which were referred to as "running horses." The running horses would have included breeds such as the Irish Hobby, the Norfolk Roadster, and the Galloway crossed with Spanish and Italian bloodlines.

The first great British racehorse was "Flying Childers," sired by the Darley Arabian—born in 1715, he was never beaten. He passed on his winning

streak to his great-great-nephew, Eclipse, who was born in 1764 and created one of the four main Thoroughbred lines.

British breeders started to keep track of pedigrees and, as this became increasingly important, the *Introduction to a General Stud Book* was published in 1791 with Volume I of the *General Stud Book* in 1808. A horse is classed as a Thoroughbred if both its parents are entered in the *General Studbook* or in the equivalent official Thoroughbred studbooks in other countries.

The Thoroughbred was originally bred to race on the flat and this today remains the main reason for the breeding. The most valuable racehorses are those that show potential as winners as three-year-olds over 1–1¾ miles (1.6–2.8 km); these races are called "Classics" such as the Derby or the Kentucky.

Another category is the National Hunt racehorse; these are raced over fences and hurdles and are usually the

later-maturing, larger Thoroughbreds with great stamina and toughness. Thoroughbreds are now specifically bred for the different race types, although plenty of flat-bred horses go on into National Hunt racing. They are also used for other sporting disciplines such as hunting, show jumping, dressage, and eventing.

CHARACTERISTICS

The best Thoroughbreds have a refined head, with large, bold eyes. The Arab influence can sometimes be seen in the slight dishing of the face. The neck is arched and elegant, leading to pronounced withers and a long sloping shoulder that helps to give the ground covering stride. The back is short, with muscular quarters. The chest and girth are deep, giving plenty of room for the heart and lungs. The legs should be clean and hard. However, defects are often found in the legs and hooves, such as lack of bone, poor horn quality, collapsed heels, and thin soles.

FULL OF PRESENCE
The Thoroughbred is a handsome horse: alert, spirited, and full of presence. He has endless courage and immense stamina. His ground covering stride at the gallop makes him the fastest breed of horse in the world.

RETRAINING With over 16,000 racehorses owned in the United Kingdom alone there is a great need for the rehabilitation and retraining of horses from the track who retire either through injury or poor performance.

BIG BUSINESS Betting turnover in the United Kingdom alone is £5 billion. At Tattersalls, the United Kingdom's biggest auction house for Thoroughbreds, 4,737 horses were sold in 2005 for a total of £185,518,800.

Trakehner

ORIGIN Poland
ENVIRONMENT
BLOOD 🜄
USES
HEIGHT 16.0–16.2 hh (64–66 in)
COLORS Any solid color

The Trakehner is one of the oldest warmbloods and is also the most refined and closest to the Thoroughbred in quality and stamp. As well as being a successful performance horse in its own right, it has been used to a great extent to upgrade and refine many other European sports horse breeds.

BLACK   BROWN   CHESTNUT   GRAY   BAY

ORIGINS

The area that is now part of Poland but which used to be East Prussia was colonized by the Order of Teutonic Knights. They established the Trakehnen stud and used native ponies as a base. These were the tough, hardy Schweiken Ponies, descendants of Poland's Konik Pony, which itself is descended from the Tarpan. In 1732, the Royal Trakehner Stud Administration was founded by King Frederick William I of Prussia. Using Danish, Turkish, and Thoroughbred stallions on the native mares, a quality coach horse was developed. From the early 1800s,

to meet the need for a more refined cavalry horse for the Prussian army, a number of Arab and Thoroughbred stallions were imported to upgrade the breed now known as the East Prussian or Trakehner. The Trakehner studbook was established in 1878. Of all the Thoroughbred blood used to develop the breed, the greatest influence was that of "Perfectionist"—an English Thoroughbred by "Persimmon," winner of the Derby and St. Ledger in 1896. A son of Perfectionist was "Tempelhüter" who produced a particularly good line of horses that is recognized as the foundation stock of the modern Trakehner breed. His influence was on the dam line as well as a direct sire. The "Dingle" line, which was equally influential in the breed's development, was based very much on Tempelhüter's daughters. Trakehners were dominating the sports horse scene as early as 1936, with the German team being mounted mainly on Trakehners to win every equestrian medal at the 1936 Berlin Olympics.

The Royal Trakehnen Stud had to be evacuated during World War II. As the Russians advanced during the winter of 1944, brave efforts were made to evacuate the breed to safety. Up to 25,000 horses, including mares and foals, set off on a trek of 900 miles (1,450 km) westward to

ABDULLAH One of the most successful Trakehners was "Abdullah." This stallion competed for the United States, winning team gold and individual silver Olympics medals in 1984. The following year he won show jumping's World Cup.

Germany. Fewer than 2,000 reached safety, but the breed was saved by the efforts of many of the original breeders. Using the original studbook, they tracked down the survivors and re-registered them in West Germany. Breeding resumed and the Trakehner quickly regained its prominence as a successful sports horse.

CHARACTERISTICS

The head of the Trakehner is full of quality, reflecting his Thoroughbred and Arab bloodlines. He has good strong limbs, stands close to the ground, and has good, hard feet.

The shoulders are well shaped and defined, and overall the horse is well balanced and agile.

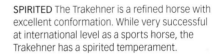

SPIRITED The Trakehner is a refined horse with excellent conformation. While very successful at international level as a sports horse, the Trakehner has a spirited temperament.

SPORTS HORSE The Trakehner has excelled in all three main equestrian disciplines. Many of the other warmblood breeds have traditionally lacked the speed required for the sport of three-day eventing, but the Trakehner has plenty of speed and scope, as well as great freedom of movement.

American Shetland

ORIGIN United States
ENVIRONMENT
BLOOD
USES
HEIGHT Up to 46 in
COLORS All colors

Shetland Ponies were first imported to North America from the Scottish Shetland Islands in the mid-1800s to haul coal from the mines. The American Shetland Pony Club was formed in 1888 to record all the Shetland Ponies being imported from Europe. It is the oldest horse registry in the United States.

BLACK   BROWN   CHESTNUT   DUN   GRAY   BAY   PALOMINO   COLORED

ORIGINS AND CHARACTERISTICS

The modern American Shetland bears no resemblance to Shetland Ponies from Scotland. It was produced by crossing finer Shetland Ponies with small Hackney Ponies, and then introducing a small amount of Thoroughbred and Arab blood.

The modern American Shetland is much more like a miniature Hackney. It moves with elegance and cadence; the influence of the Hackney is very clear in the high-stepping action. The head is refined, and some have the characteristics of the Arab. They tend to be long and narrow through the back, with long, fine, clean legs. The hooves are generally neat and hard.

The American Shetland Pony Club has two studbooks: Division A is for ponies with 12.5 percent or less outcross blood; and Division B is open to any pony with 12.5 percent or more outcross blood. Foundation Certificates go to ponies from four generations of Division A breeding.

SHOWING CLASS Showing classes for the American Shetland Pony are divided into height divisions: under 43", and 43" to 46". The classes include "in-hand," and "performance," which includes roadster, harness, and pleasure driving.

Bashkir

ORIGIN Russia
ENVIRONMENT
BLOOD
USES
HEIGHT 13.0–14.0 hh (52–56 in)
COLORS Chestnut, bay, or palomino

CHESTNUT   BAY   PALOMINO

The Bashkir is an ancient breed that has lived for thousands of years in the Ural Mountains, in the former Soviet Union. They are probably related to the steppe horses of western Asia, and may contain other influences probably of Turkish origin. In 1845, government breeding centers were set up to improve the stock for agricultural purposes, including meat and milk.

ORIGINS

Two types of pony were developed: The mountain type, which is more suitable for riding; and the heavier steppe variety, often used for light draft and other farm work.

Bashkir endurance is legendary; it is claimed that a Bashkir Troika (carriage/sleigh) can cover 75–85 miles (120–140 km) a day in the snow. The breed is hardy and the herds live out in deep snow and

BASHKIR CURLY
The Bashkir was originally sought-after by Native Americans. Today they are gaining popularity in the United States with over 1,000 registered Bashkir Curlies in the country.

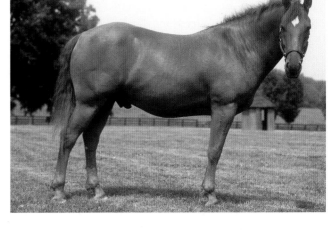

blizzard conditions at temperatures that fall between 14 and -40 degrees Fahrenheit (between -10 and -40 degrees centigrade).

The "Bashkir Curly" is a United States breed. Some insist that

it is related to the Russian Bashkir while others say that it is not. It remains a mystery how these ponies came to the United States, but they are gaining in popularity. It is understood that they were first sought-after by Native Americans living in the northwestern states.

CHARACTERISTICS

The Bashkir Pony's legs are short and strong with very hard hooves that are capable of dealing with the rough terrain of Russia's Ural Mountains. The mane and tail of the Bashkir Pony tend to be curly and full, and its winter coat is similarly curly and very thick. The hair can be combed, spun, and then woven to produce cloth. Interestingly, people who suffer allergies to horses can wear the cloth made from this pony's coat.

HEAVY HEADED PONY
The Bashkir has a heavy head, which is straight in profile with bright eyes. The long neck leads to a deep chest and sloping shoulders. The withers are low, and sometimes the back can be dipped and the tail low set.

Camargue

ORIGIN France
ENVIRONMENT
BLOOD
USES
HEIGHT 13.1–14.1 hh (53–57 in)
COLORS Gray

The indigenous white horses of the Camargue, in the Rhône delta of southern France, are also called "the horses of the sea." The harshness of their environment and their isolation from outside influences have made them very distinctive. They are the traditional mounts of the Camargue herdsmen but are finding a new role as trekking ponies for tourists.

ORIGINS

The Camargue has only been officially recognized since 1968, but there is no doubt it is an ancient breed, possibly prehistoric. It is similar in size and proportions to the skeletons of the prehistoric horses found at Solutré. This area of France would have seen many armies come and go and each would have brought horses that could have bred with the native Camargue. A strong Barb input may have occurred as a result of Moorish invasions in the 7th and 8th centuries, and prior to this there could have been Asian and Mongol influences.

WELL MADE The main failing is in the short, straight shoulder, but otherwise the Camargue is compact and muscular, with excellent limbs and feet.

CHARACTERISTICS

The herds of "white" horses running freely through the saltwater marshes are a beautiful sight, although on closer inspection the Camargue is a little plain. His primitive origins show in the heavy, slightly coarse head, but he is an exceptionally strong, sound, and hardy little horse.

BULL PONY The Camargue is the traditional mount of the guardians of the herds of bulls, which also roam the Camargue region.

Caspian

ORIGIN Iran
ENVIRONMENT
BLOOD
USES
HEIGHT 10.0–11.0 hh (40–44 in)
COLORS All solid colors

The Caspian is classified as a pony because of its size, but it has all the refinement and proportions of a horse. In 1965, a small herd of "miniature horses" was found at Amol in northern Iran, in a mountainous area close to the Caspian Sea. They are believed to be related to the small horses depicted on ancient artifacts.

BLACK

BROWN

CHESTNUT

GRAY

BAY

ORIGINS AND CHARACTERISTICS

Since the Caspian's rediscovery, bones of its early antecedents, dating back to over 3,000 years ago, have also been unearthed in Iran.

It has long been accepted that just prior to domestication, four subspecies of horse had evolved. The Type 4 horse was the smallest yet most refined of this group with a distinctive concave profile and highset tail. This is believed to be the ancestor of the Caspian. A breeding program was set up to maintain and protect the breed, and it is now bred in many countries.

The Caspian's skeleton has several unique features: It has an extra molar on each side of the upper jaw and the bones of its head and scapula are different in form to those of other horses.

The Caspian has a gracefully arched neck, sloping shoulders, and defined withers. The body is slim and the tail is high set. The limbs are slender but strong, and the feet are hard and sound.

AGILE AND ATHLETIC Despite its small stature, the Caspian has the ground-covering stride of a horse and is also an exceptionally talented jumper. It has a kind and willing nature, and is also very intelligent.

Chincoteague

ORIGIN United States
ENVIRONMENT
BLOOD 🟢
USES 🐎 🐴
HEIGHT 14.2 hh (58 in)
COLORS Colored or roan

COLORED   ROAN

Named after the island they live on, Chincoteague Ponies are small and hardy. It is believed their ancestors swam to the island from a Spanish ship that had capsized off the coast in 1600. To survive, they had to live off coarse grasses and drink salt water. This foundation stock evolved into the breed known today.

ORIGINS AND CHARACTERISTICS
Two groups of ponies have descended from the original 17 Arab Horses that survived the shipwreck: The Maryland herd, and the Virginia herd. The Virginia herd is larger and is managed by the Volunteer Fire Department. The Maryland herd is more feral, and is owned and cared for by the United States Parks Authority.

The Chincoteague Pony is a very good doer. It is well proportioned, strong, and muscular. The pony has a good, kind nature, and seems to love being around people.

CHILD'S PONY The Chincoteague makes a good child's pony, excelling in American show classes, as well as jumping and driving.

Connemara

ORIGIN Ireland
ENVIRONMENT 🌾
BLOOD 🟢
USES 🐎 🐴 🐎
HEIGHT 13.0–14.2 hh (52–58 in)
COLORS All colors, but predominantly gray

BLACK   BROWN   CHESTNUT   GRAY   ROAN

The Connemara is named after a small area in the Connaught region of Western Ireland. The habitat is bleak, bordered on one side by Galway Bay, and on the other by the Atlantic Ocean. This is Ireland's only indigenous breed and it has had to be tough to survive. It is an exceptional performance pony.

ORIGINS AND CHARACTERISTICS
This breed may have originated from imported Barb and Spanish horses that bred with the native stock, or it may have evolved from stock brought to Ireland by the Celts, including Icelandic, Shetland, and Norwegian Fjord Ponies. Its quality would suggest that, either way, it has been influenced by Spanish or Arab blood.

The Connemara is an athletic pony and is free, fluent, and true in its paces, excelling in all competitive disciplines. It makes an ideal child's pony, and is popular with small adults.

GRAY COLOR The Connemara Pony is predominantly gray; dun and palomino were once common, but are now very rarely seen.

Dales Pony

ORIGIN United Kingdom

ENVIRONMENT

BLOOD

USES

HEIGHT 13.2–14.2 hh (54–58 in)

COLORS Predominantly black, with some brown, gray, bay, or, rarely, roan

| BLACK | BROWN | GRAY | BAY | ROAN |

The Dales Pony originates from northern England on the hills of the Pennines, and it gets its name from the river valleys. The foundation stock is believed to be Scottish Galloway. The Dales shares a lot of its ancestry with its close neighbor the Fell Pony. The Friesian influences both breeds.

STUDBOOKS The Dales Pony studbook was opened in 1916. However, World War II meant that selective breeding was limited and, by 1955, only four ponies remained registered.

employed mainly for riding and carriage driving, competing successfully in a wide range of disciplines.

CHARACTERISTICS

The attractive Dales Pony has a neat, intelligent head with bright eyes that are set well apart. The ears curve slightly inward. The long, strong neck leads to muscular, sloping shoulders. The withers should not be too fine. The body is compact, deep through the chest, and has well-sprung ribs. The hindquarters are extremely powerful, with well-developed and muscular second thighs. The strong legs show plenty of flexibility but should have no coarseness.

ORIGINS

The Dales Pony is predominantly black in color. Over the centuries, the breed has been crossed with, first, the Norfolk Roadster, and later, during the 19th century, Welsh Cobs and Clydesdales.

The Dales was originally used as a pack pony, particularly in the lead mining industries. As the mines became more mechanized, its ability to haul loads of over a ton, to plow, and also drive to market in style made the Dales a firm favorite with farmers. Later, the pace of the Dales made it popular as a light carriage horse, providing a speedy means of transportation. Today, it is

LONG MANE The Dales Pony has silky feathering on its legs, and an abundance of mane and tail hair.

Dartmoor

ORIGIN United Kingdom

ENVIRONMENT

BLOOD 🜄

USES

HEIGHT 12.2 hh (50 in) and under

COLORS Traditionally black, brown, or bay, but occasionally dun or gray

| BLACK | BROWN | DUN | GRAY | BAY |

Ponies have been running free on the moorlands of Dartmoor in southwest England for centuries. The earliest reference to them was in the 11th century. Over time they served as pack ponies, being used for light farm and carriage work and, today, they are bred for the show ring and as general riding ponies for children.

ORIGINS

The exact origins of the breed are not known. They inhabit a wild and harsh environment, but not in a particularly isolated area since they lived on the path of an important trade route between Plymouth and Exeter. This would have led to the breed being easily influenced by other bloodlines. Some of the Arab and Barb horses brought back to England by the crusaders could have escaped onto the moors, and the 19th century saw the introduction of trotting, Thoroughbred, Welsh Pony, Cob, and Exmoor blood.

PART-BREDS There are many part-bred ponies on the moor today, leading to a range of shapes, sizes, and colors. The Dartmoor Pony Society carries a Part-Bred Dartmoor register open to ponies by a licensed stallion and which have at least 25 percent Dartmoor blood. One parent or grandparent must be a registered Dartmoor.

Certainly, the bleak and rugged nature of the moorland shaped the stamp of pony most likely to survive on it. There is very little shelter to be found on the moors; the landscape is undulating but open to the weather from all directions. Larger ponies are distinctly disadvantaged by the lack of shelter. The first studbook was opened in 1899 and allowed for ponies up to 14 hh (56 in) for "political" rather than practical reasons. At the time, in 1898, the Polo Pony studbook was eager to make use of the native breeds as foundation stock for Polo Ponies. A larger pony would be needed for this purpose, which is why attempts were made to encourage the larger type. But, in 1899, when the ponies were gathered up and brought in for inspection and entry in the studbook, three-quarters of them were 12.2 hh (50 in) or under! In 1924, the height limit was reset at 12.2 hh (50 in) in recognition of the forces of nature.

Dartmoor Ponies are often bred in the "comfort" of private studs, and many of the ponies on the moor today are crossbreds. There is a risk that random crossbreeding and breeding

"off the moor" will lead to the loss of some of the pony's hardiness and characteristics. To encourage the continuation of purebred ponies on the moor, there is a scheme whereby approved mares are kept in fenced off areas of the moor called "newtakes," where they run with a purebred Dartmoor stallion.

CHARACTERISTICS

The Dartmoor should have a small, relatively fine head, with large, kind eyes and small ears. As he is primarily a riding pony, the neck of the Dartmoor should be a good length. The shoulders must be well laid and sloping. The body should be strong and deep, and of medium length. Most of the ponies originally entered in the studbook were black, brown, or bay, with just a handful of grays and duns in existence. Today, there are many more color variations. There was originally very little to be seen in the way of white markings. Some carried a white star, or white spot on the nose, with maybe the occasional white fetlock. White markings continue to be discouraged by the breed society today.

SOUND BREED The rugged moorland terrain has led to the development of a tough, sound pony. The limbs have plenty of bone, with short, flat, hard cannon bones. The forearm and second thigh should be muscular, and the feet are well shaped and hard.

PUREBRED DARTMOOR PONIES To encourage purebred stock, a selection of mares is kept with a registered purebred Dartmoor stallion in enclosures called "newtakes." The offspring produced are inspected and, if approved, are entered in a supplementary studbook. Over time, as they are bred again to a purebred stallion, the offspring will be eligible for entry as registered purebred Dartmoors.

Exmoor

ORIGIN United Kingdom
ENVIRONMENT 🌾
BLOOD 💧
USES 🐎 🛷 🐴
HEIGHT 12.2–13.3 hh (50–55 in)
COLORS Bay, brown, or dun

BROWN

DUN

BAY

The Exmoor is the oldest of the United Kingdom's mountain and moorland breeds, having roamed on Exmoor since the Bronze Age, 4,000 years ago. The earliest breed records can be traced back to 1820, but the breed society was not formed until 1921. They are branded on the shoulder with a star and herd number; on the nearside hindquarters is the pony's unique number.

ORIGINS AND CHARACTERISTICS

Herds of ponies still run wild today on Exmoor, although numbers are not huge. The robust build and constitution of the Exmoor makes it an ideal riding and driving pony. Correctly handled, it also makes an excellent first pony for a child, as well as being a good all-around performance pony for the older child or small adult. When crossed with Thoroughbreds, they make very useful competition horses.

The Exmoor has a clean-cut face, with a broad forehead. He has a good length of neck with well-laid shoulders. He has a powerful body with a deep chest. The legs are short and clean with small, strong feet.

HOME-BRED PONY If bred away from Exmoor, the breed tends to lose type. The purity of the breed requires a return to breeding from ponies on the moor in order to retain its ancient characteristics.

HEAVY EYELIDS A noticeable characteristic of the Exmoor pony is its pale-colored muzzle. It has large eyes that have heavy upper eyelids. Like the muzzle, the eyes are surrounded by lighter colored hair.

Falabella

ORIGIN Argentina
ENVIRONMENT 🌾
BLOOD 🌢
USES Novelty
HEIGHT 7.0 hh (28 in)
COLORS All colors

The Falabella is a miniature breed developed near Buenos Aires, in Argentina, by the Falabella family. They crossed the smallest Shetland with a very small Thoroughbred, and continued to breed from the smallest offspring. Unfortunately, this process has caused conformational defects.

 BLACK
 BROWN
 CHESTNUT
 DUN
 GRAY
 BAY
 PALOMINO
 COLORED

ORIGINS AND CHARACTERISTICS

The International Falabella Miniature Horse Society maintains a breed registry to insure that the breed remains pure. However, conformational defects are common, such as weak, straight hocks, crooked limbs and heavy heads, often with a ewe neck. The breed has also lost the inherent toughness and vigor that is characteristic of the Shetland Pony.

A Falabella should have a head similar to a Shetland Pony and, ideally, the head should be in proportion to its body. Overall, a Falabella should have the proportions of a horse. Since it first developed, many different breeds have been used to produce the Falabella and, as a consequence, they come in many interesting colors including spotted patterns and skewbalds.

The foals are very small when born, just 16 in (40 cm), but they grow quickly in their first year. They have two fewer vertebrae and ribs than a normal horse or pony.

MINI HORSES Falabellas have the appearance of scaled-down horses rather than ponies. Although rare, they continue to be bred in Argentina, and also in the United Kingdom.

The Falabella is friendly and intelligent, and thrives on attention. It requires regular grooming, care, and attention and usually needs to wear blankets during cold weather.

The Falabella tends to be kept as a pet since it is too small for riding or for any other purpose, although they are occasionally seen in harness. They are delicate and need looking after like a Thoroughbred Horse.

MINIATURE PET Falabellas are often shown in hand at breed shows, where they will be judged on conformation, temperament, and movement. They are no bigger than an average-sized dog.

Fell Pony

ORIGIN United Kingdom
ENVIRONMENT
BLOOD 💧
USES 🐎 🐴
HEIGHT 14.0 hh (56 in)
COLORS Black, brown, gray, or bay

The Fell is related to the Dales Pony and the Friesian. Some trotting blood has been added, and the breed was used in harness in the 18th and 19th centuries. The Fell is lighter than the Dales, although the distinction was only recognized in 1916 when the two breed societies formed.

BLACK

BROWN

GRAY

BAY

VERSATILE When crossed with a Thoroughbred, the Fell Pony makes an excellent versatile competition horse.

ORIGINS AND CHARACTERISTICS

The Friesian and the extinct Galloway were the main influences on the Fell. The Galloway was a swift, strong mount, used by raiding Celts as well as Scottish drovers.

A fast active walk and trot makes the Fell an excellent carriage horse. It is able to carry up to 220 pounds (100 kg), which makes its a popular

ROYAL PONIES Queen Elizabeth of the United Kingdom is an enthusiastic breeder of Fells and, for many years, HRH Prince Phillip has competed with a team in horse-driving trials, which involve dressage, a marathon with obstacles, and a course of cones.

choice among farmers as a hunter; it is also a reliable packhorse.

The head is small and well set on the neck, with a broad forehead and bright and prominent eyes. It has a good, sloping shoulder that makes the paces comfortable, and has a strong, deep body with muscular loins. The hindquarters are strong with a well-set tail. It has strong limbs with good, flat bone below the knee.

The strong neck is longer than that of the Dales, giving a better length of reins, which is very desirable in a riding horse.

Hackney Pony

ORIGIN United Kingdom
ENVIRONMENT
BLOOD ◊
USES
HEIGHT 12.2–14.0 hh (50–56 in)
COLORS Black, brown, or bay

BLACK   BROWN   BAY

The Hackney Pony is a small version of the Hackney Horse, both based on the Norfolk and Yorkshire Roadsters. Christopher Wilson, who crossed his Roadster stallion with Fell mares, started this pony version, which is exported and exhibited all over the world.

ORIGINS AND CHARACTERISTICS

The key feature of the Hackney Pony is the high knee action, which should be fluent with the foot flung forward in a rounded movement. The hocks should come well underneath the body. The Hackney Pony has a small and intelligent head, a long neck, powerful shoulders, and a compact body. He is full of courage and has great stamina.

TEST Hackney Ponies compete in driving classes where they are judged on conformation, action, and manners.

Haflinger

ORIGIN Austria
ENVIRONMENT ▲
BLOOD ◊
USES 🐎 🐎
HEIGHT 14.0 hh (56 in)
COLORS Chestnut

The Haflinger Pony is sturdy and good natured, making it popular with the Austrian hill farmers. It has been used as a packhorse during times of peace and war. Just before World War II, the German government promoted the breed as a means of transportation in the mountains.

ORIGINS AND CHARACTERISTICS

The attractive and popular Haflinger Pony is named after the Austrian village of Hafling in the South Tyrol mountains. His exact breeding is uncertain, but the first written evidence was in 1868 when the stallion "El Bedavi XXII" was used to improve local herds. Over the years, inbreeding has resulted in a distinctive pony, particularly remarked upon for its chestnut color and flaxen mane and tail.

BRAND MARK Haflingers that are registered in the studbook are branded with an edelweiss flower with an "H" in the center.

Highland

ORIGIN United Kingdom
ENVIRONMENT
BLOOD 💧
USES 🐎 🐎
HEIGHT 13.0–14.2 hh (52–58 in)
COLORS Commonly dun, but also black, brown, chestnut, gray, or bay

The Highland is one of the strongest and heaviest of the mountain and moorland breeds in the United Kingdom. It has had input from both Arab and Clydesdale blood. The Dukes of Atholl have been influential breeders, and they introduced Oriental blood as early as the 16th century.

BLACK

BROWN

CHESTNUT

DUN

GRAY

BAY

STRIKING The striking coloring features varying shades of dun, usually with a dorsal stripe—a sign of primitive breeding.

IN DEMAND The Highland has a broad face, with kind eyes. The head is carried high on a strong, arched neck. He is in demand today, especially on the sporting estates in Scotland, where he is used to carry game panniers.

ORIGINS

In the early 16th century, some Percherons were given to King James II of Scotland by Louis XII of France. These, along with Spanish horses, were used to upgrade the native stock of ponies. The resultant Highland Pony used to vary from area to area, with the smaller and faster Highland coming from the Western Isles and heavier ponies coming from the mainland. The Highland Pony Society, which was formed in 1923, no longer recognizes these distinctions, which have been largely lost with crossbreeding.

The Highland Pony is versatile, being used both as a pack and a riding horse, and he can be found competing in driving as well as dressage. Crossed with a Thoroughbred, the Highland makes an excellent hunter and event horse.

CHARACTERISTICS

The sturdy Highland has laid-back shoulders and a compact body. The hindquarters are powerful with well-developed thighs and second thighs. The cannon bones are short and strong. The Highland has light feathering but a long, flowing, silky mane and tail. Most show a dorsal stripe and some have "primitive" zebra markings on the legs.

Icelandic Pony

ORIGIN Iceland
ENVIRONMENT
BLOOD
USES
HEIGHT 12.3–13.2 hh (51–54 in)
COLORS All colors

The isolation of the Icelandic makes him one of the purest breeds in the world. The small, sturdy horses that were his ancestors were taken to Iceland from Norway and Britain by settlers as early as the 9th century. A law passed in 930AD forbade the importation of more horses, so the breed has hardly changed since the Vikings.

BLACK   BROWN   CHESTNUT   DUN   GRAY   BAY   PALOMINO   COLORED

ORIGINS AND CHARACTERISTICS

Apart from its natural evolution in its harsh environment, the Icelandic Pony has been the subject of selective breeding since 1879. Selection trials were first held at Skagafjordur, Iceland's

BUILT TO WORK The diminutive Icelandic Pony has enormous strength and can carry a full-grown man for many hours without a problem.

main breeding area. Conformation is taken into account, but the main criterion is the quality of the horse's paces. The Icelandic Pony has five distinct paces: The fetgangur (walk), the brokk (trot), the stokk (gallop), the skeid (a rapid lateral pace), and the most famous of all, the tolt (a running walk that is used when covering rough terrain).

TOUGH LITTLE PONY The pony has a heavy head, which it carries well on a good neck. The deep body ends in muscular hindquarters.

Konik Pony

ORIGIN Poland
ENVIRONMENT
BLOOD 🌢
USES 🐕 🏇 🐎 🐎 🐎
HEIGHT 13.0 hh (52 in)
COLORS Dun

Although technically a pony, the Konik has many horse-like characteristics. The Konik's relationship with ancient breeds is revealed in the primitive dorsal stripe, and sometimes transverse zebra stripes on the legs.

ORIGINS AND CHARACTERISTICS

The Konik Pony's resemblance to the Tarpan clearly illustrates how closely related it is to that primitive horse. Although the Konik Pony has long been produced throughout Poland, breeding is now centered at the state studs in the Rzeszow province, and a uniform type of pony has existed for many years.

The head is large, with a short, strong neck. The shoulders are upright, giving a short stride. With low withers and a wide body, the legs are strong but tend to have "cow" hocks.

TARPAN COPY
Konik mares are sometimes bred to Przewalski Horses, and the result is an animal even more similar than the Konik itself to its forefather, the Tarpan.

Miniature Horse

ORIGIN Worldwide
ENVIRONMENT 🌵 🌲 ⛰ 🌾 🌿
BLOOD 🌢
USES Pets
HEIGHT Less than 39 in
COLORS All colors

The Miniature Horse is bred all over the world, using many different small breeds, including the Shetland and Dartmoor. The designation of a Miniature Horse for breed registration is dependent solely on its height, which is usually less than 39 in (1 m).

BLACK	BROWN	CHESTNUT	DUN	GRAY	COLORED

ORIGINS AND CHARACTERISTICS

During the 17th century, Miniature Horses were bred as pets for Europe's nobility. However, some were used as pit ponies, particularly in Wales and northern Europe.

Miniature Horses are friendly and interact well with people. They are often kept as pets, although they must be treated as an equine. In the United States they are trained to be "service" animals, playing a similar role to that of guide dogs.

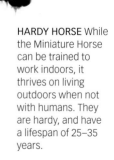

HARDY HORSE While the Miniature Horse can be trained to work indoors, it thrives on living outdoors when not with humans. They are hardy, and have a lifespan of 25–35 years.

New Forest Pony

ORIGIN United Kingdom
ENVIRONMENT
BLOOD
USES
HEIGHT 13.2–14.2 hh (54–58 in)
COLORS All solid colors

The New Forest Pony still runs free in the woodland and common land of the New Forest in Hampshire, England. The ponies are a great tourist attraction, and they are friendly and trainable by nature. An annual "drift" (roundup) is used to sort out those to be sold and those to remain in the forest as breeding stock.

BLACK   BROWN   CHESTNUT   DUN   GRAY   BAY

MADE FOR RIDING The New Forest Pony is popular throughout Europe as a children's riding and competition pony.

CHARACTERISTICS

The New Forest Pony is renowned as being a good child's riding pony, although he is also sturdy enough to carry an adult. The attractive head is more horse-like than that of most ponies, but it is the shoulders that are particularly noteworthy, being long and sloping, giving the pony a long, low, easy action. As with all native ponies, the New Forest is surefooted, tough, and sound.

ORIGINS

Ponies have run wild in the New Forest since the passing of Canute's Forest Law in 1016. The New Forest Pony that we recognize today has certainly achieved a uniformity of type despite its very mixed ancestry. Welsh Ponies were introduced in the 12th century, and high class stallions ran with the mares for a while, including the Thoroughbred "Marske," famed as the sire of the greatest racehorse of all time, "Eclipse"!

HORSEY HEAD The head of the New Forest Pony is more like that of a horse, with a broad forehead and narrow muzzle.

Norwegian Fjord

ORIGIN Norway
ENVIRONMENT ▲
BLOOD ⬦
USES 🐎 🐎
HEIGHT 13.0–14.0 hh (52–56 in)
COLORS Dun

The Norwegian Fjord is an instantly recognizable pony with his distinctive dun coloring and striking bicolored mane and tail. He is believed to have inhabited his homeland since prehistoric times, and bears a strong resemblance to the Asiatic Wild Horse. A black dorsal stripe runs from the forelock to the tip of the tail.

ORIGINS

The Fjord Pony is believed to be related to both the Asiatic Wild Horse and the Tarpan. The overall shape and coloring is very similar to the Asiatic Wild Horse, but he is more refined than that particular ancestor, indicating a link to the Tarpan also. The Fjord Pony is depicted in Viking carvings, and it was the Vikings who began the tradition of cutting the mane in a distinctive crescent shape, with the central dark hair standing out above the silver. The harsh and arduous mountain landscape has helped to create a pony that is very strong, hardy, and surefooted. He has proved to be a great workhorse to the Norwegians, plowing difficult terrain and easily negotiating steep, hazardous mountain tracks as a packhorse.

CHARACTERISTICS

The Fjord has a typical pony head, with small ears, wide-set eyes, and a narrow, light-colored muzzle. The neck is thick and strong, and the body barrel-like with a broad chest. There is little definition through the shoulders and withers, but overall he is a perfect little powerhouse of strength. The limbs are exceptionally good, being short and strong, with good joints and plenty of bone. The feet are very hard and well shaped. Today, the pony is popular in countries outside Norway, proving itself an excellent little riding and driving pony. He is popular as a riding pony not only because he is sound and surefooted but also because he is very attractive.

ACTIVE MOVER Popular for both riding and driving, the Fjord Pony has the good, active paces, particularly in trot, so often found in mountain breeds. The distinctive dun coloring seen here is always paired with the unique silver-and-black mane and tail.

WILLING WORKER The Norwegian Fjord has a kind, and willing temperament although, like most tough pony breeds, he will sometimes have his own opinions about life.

Shetland Pony

ORIGIN United Kingdom
ENVIRONMENT
BLOOD 💧
USES 🏇 🛒 🐎
HEIGHT Under 42 in
COLORS All colors except spotted

The Shetland is the smallest of the United Kingdom's natives, but is probably one of the best known worldwide. There have been ponies on the Scottish Shetland Islands for centuries, although their exact origin is not known. Despite their stature, they have greater strength relative to their size than most other equines.

BLACK

BROWN

CHESTNUT

DUN

GRAY

BAY

SMALL WONDER The Shetland Pony has a small but broad head and an intelligent eye. Large nasal cavities allow air to be warmed before entering the lungs.

CHARACTER The strong character of the Shetland Pony is legendary. Though small, they are strong-minded and will not be dominated, as many a young rider has found out.

ORIGINS AND CHARACTERISTICS

The Shetland Pony probably descends from the primitive Tundra-type horse, descendants of which were probably brought to the Shetland Islands over 10,000 years ago. The isolation of the islands, as well as the bleak and harsh environment, would have shaped the evolution of these early animals. The Shetland Islands offer little shelter and sparse grazing; so the smaller the animal, the more chance he has of finding sufficient food and shelter.

Welsh Pony (Section A)

ORIGIN United Kingdom

ENVIRONMENT

BLOOD

USES

HEIGHT 12.0 hh (48 in)

COLORS All solid colors, including dun and palomino

The Welsh Section A, also known as the Welsh Mountain Pony, is probably the most well-known and numerous of the British mountain and moorland ponies. It is considered by many to be the most beautiful of all the pony breeds. It is the base from which the three other divisions of Welsh Pony and Cob evolve.

BLACK	BROWN	CHESTNUT	DUN	GRAY	BAY	PALOMINO	ROAN

ORIGINS

The evolution of the breed is vague, but it goes back, at least, to Roman times. The Romans crossed the native Celtic ponies with horses of eastern origin. More recently, in the 18th century, the breed was enhanced with the use of Thoroughbred, Arab, and Barb blood.

MOUNTAIN PONIES The Welsh Mountain Pony still roams the moors and mountains of Wales. This insures that the pony remains hardy and thrifty, and strong and nimble.

CHARACTERISTICS

The head is small and set well on a neck of good length, and carried well on gently sloping shoulders. The withers are clearly defined, and the limbs are set square. It moves quickly and freely, with good hocks, and knees that flex well. It is popular as a child's pony since it is a good jumper and excels in the show ring. It is becoming increasingly popular as a carriage-driving pony, especially in the competitive world of driving trials, in which speed and agility play important roles.

PURE BEAUTY The eastern influence is still clearly visible in today's Welsh Mountain Pony with its elegant head and slightly dished face, large, alert eyes, and wide, flared nostrils.

Welsh Pony (Section B)

ORIGIN United Kingdom
ENVIRONMENT
BLOOD
USES
HEIGHT 13.2 hh (54 in)
COLORS All solid colors, including dun and palomino

The Welsh Section B, or Welsh Pony, is a more modern and slightly larger version of the Welsh Section A. Originally bred by the Welsh hill farmers to provide a means of transportation and for herding livestock, in more recent years it has developed into an ideal pony for children.

BLACK   BROWN   CHESTNUT   DUN   GRAY   BAY   PALOMINO   ROAN

ORIGINS
The Welsh Section B pony is very similar to the Welsh Section A, but the fact that it is slightly larger makes it a more versatile riding pony. It was bred from the Welsh Mountain Pony, using Welsh Cob, Thoroughbred, and Arab blood, and is generally taller and lighter in build than the Welsh Mountain Pony.

CONFORMATION The conformation of the Section B Pony is similar to that of the slightly smaller Section A Pony, with a good length of neck and sloping shoulders.

BRED WITH CARE The Welsh Pony and Cob Society was founded in 1901 to oversee the development of the four divisions of Welsh ponies.

CHARACTERISTICS
Its agility, balance, and speed made it an ideal pony for the hill farmer to check and move livestock. The legs are set square and are strong with short cannons. These attributes, combined with its natural talent for jumping and its good nature, have also made it an ideal competition pony for the younger rider. It is also highly sought-after for both pleasure and competitive carriage driving.

Welsh Pony (Section C)

ORIGIN United Kingdom
ENVIRONMENT ▲
BLOOD ◊
USES 🐎 🐎
HEIGHT 13.2 hh (54 in)
COLORS Black, brown, chestnut, dun, gray, bay, or palomino

The Welsh Section C is also referred to as the Welsh Pony of Cob Type. It is the smaller of the two Welsh Cobs, the other being the Section D. This stocky pony has also been called the "farm pony," since they were used for all types of farm work on the Welsh hills, as well as being used in the slate mines of North Wales.

 BLACK
 BROWN
 CHESTNUT
 DUN
 GRAY
 BAY
 PALOMINO

ORIGINS AND CHARACTERISTICS

Originally, this pony was usually the offspring of a Section A Pony and a small Cob. However, it is now produced by mating registered Section C Ponies.

The Welsh Pony Section C retains many of the attributes of the Welsh Section A, being tough, hardy, and sound in constitution. The neck is thick and strong, and carried high and arched. Although the withers tend to be low, the shoulders are long and the action is energetic and ground-covering. The legs are clean and strong, and there is light, silky feathering at the heels.

ELEGANT PONY Like the Welsh Sections A and B, the Welsh Section C has cadence and elegance. Its overall conformation is compact and stylish, making it popular with children and adults alike.

ACTION PONY The Welsh Section C is renowned for its ability to trot for long periods of time, covering the ground with ease and elegance. They are often shown in hand.

Welsh Pony (Section D)

ORIGIN United Kingdom
ENVIRONMENT
BLOOD
USES
HEIGHT 14.0–15.0 hh (56–60 in)
COLORS Black, brown, chestnut, dun, gray, bay, or palomino

BLACK BROWN CHESTNUT DUN GRAY BAY PALOMINO

For centuries, the Welsh hill farmers have used the Welsh Section D, also known as the Welsh Cob, as an all-around utility horse. It is believed that the Section D is influenced by the Section A and Andalucians, which were bred in the Welsh Borders during the 11th and 12th centuries.

CHARACTERISTICS
The Cob retains a pony-like head, which is full of character and quality. The ears are neat. The neck is crested and arched, and runs smoothly into strong shoulders that are nicely sloping. The body is compact, with good depth through the girth and well-sprung ribs. The legs are muscled with defined joints and a good deal of bone.

GREAT ACTION The Section D has a free action; the knee bends allowing the whole foreleg to extend straight from the shoulder and reach forward as far as possible.

ORIGINS
During the 18th and 19th centuries, the Section D was upgraded using the Norfolk Roadster and Yorkshire Coach Horses. Much sought-after as a gun horse and for mounted infantry, until 1960, the Cob was also used on milk, bread, and general delivery routes throughout Wales.

VERSATILE The Section D is popular as a riding horse; although small it is able to easily carry an adult rider. It has a natural jumping ability and is often a good competition horse.

INDEX